We Are Aging

Jack Botwinick, author of *Cognitive Processes in Maturity and Old Age* and *Aging and Behavior* (both published by Springer Publishing Co.) received his Ph.D. from New York University and has been involved in the study of adult aging most of his long professional career. He has been Professor of Psychology at Washington University in St. Louis since 1969 and Director of the Aging and Development Program of the University's Department of Psychology since 1971. He has also been Associate Professor and then Professor of Medical Psychology at Duke University Medical School. He served as president of the Division of Adult Development and Aging of the American Psychological Association and president of the behavioral division of the Gerontological Society.

In 1979, he was honored by the American Psychological Association's Division of Adult Development and Aging in their "Distinguished Contribution Award" for "outstanding scientific contributions to the psychological study of adult development and aging." In 1979 he was also given the prestigious Kleemeier Award by the Gerontological Society "in recognition of outstanding and meritorious research in the field of gerontology."

We Are Aging

Jack Botwinick

Springer Publishing Company
New York

Copyright © 1981 by Springer Publishing Company, Inc.

Springer Publishing Company, Inc.
200 Park Avenue South
New York, New York 10003

81 82 83 84 85 / 10 9 8 7 6 5 4 3 2 1

Library of Congress Cataloging in Publication Data

Botwinick, Jack.
  We are aging.

  Includes bibliographical references and index.
  1. Aged—United States.   2. Aging.   3. Old age.
I. Title.
HQ1064.U5B67   305.2'6'0973   80-27043
ISBN 0-8261-3380-0
ISBN 0-8261-3381-9 (pbk.)

Printed in the United States of America

Contents

v

Preface

Teachers in both universities and junior colleges have indicated to me that they need an up-to-date, simple-to-read, yet accurate account of social and psychological aging. *We Are Aging* is designed to fill this need. Effort was made to write this book at a reading level suitable for just about anyone who wants to learn, in a nontechnical way, more about life after the middle years. I believe this has been accomplished, except perhaps in Chapter 15 and in one or two brief sections where the content didn't allow less technical explanations. References are provided at the end of each chapter for those who want more detail and greater technical understanding.

We are aging—all of us. May we age well. If this book can play a small role in helping us to do so, I cannot think of greater gratification.

I thank Mrs. Jane Boggs who typed and retyped the various drafts of the manuscript, and I thank my wife, Joan, who gave editorial advice throughout.

Chapter 1

Aging and the Aged

Many scientists believe that aging begins at the time of birth, whereas others believe that aging begins with sexual maturity. First there is growth and development, and then development continues in some areas but declines in others. There is little argument about the decline of biological functions, but whether or not mental abilities decline in later life is controversial; there is also some debate among those who perceive a decline as to just when it begins. There is no doubt, however, that people age at different rates and in different ways.

BECOMING OLD

We are all aging, not only individually, but also as a whole population. There are more old people now than ever before. This is more true in some countries than in others, but it is true in most of the western world. This fact may not come as a surprise to many. However, it is less well known that, while we are getting older, our maximum life span, as determined by our genes, has hardly increased since biblical times, in any case not over the last 100,000 years. This may sound paradoxical, but it is simply that as time has moved on, more and more of us have lived closer to the length of life our genes have programmed for us. In other words, life expectancy has gotten closer to the maximum life span, generally considered to be between 95 and 110 years.

Biomedical progress has drastically reduced infant and child death and has led to greater control of acute diseases of young adulthood and middle age. These advances plus our improved knowledge of what is and what is not good for us have permitted our life expectancies to approach the maximum life span.

Our life expectancy has increased considerably over the years. For example, 2,000 years ago in Rome, the average length of life was about 22 years; in the late 1600s, it was about 33 years. As late as 1900, it was only about 50 years in the United States, and in 1946 it was 66. Today, a person's life expectancy is in the mid-seventies. If this trend of increasing life expectancy continues, a strange phenomenon which some scientists are predicting may occur: nearly everyone will reach the age of the maximum life span of about 95 to 110 years. Some scientists believe that death will result from amyloidosis—a faulty biochemical process involving protein metabolism.

In any case, our present life expectancy is changing the face of our society. In the United States, more than 30 percent of the people are over age 45, more than 15 percent are over 60, and about 10 percent are over 65. In 40 to 50 years we expect that the over-65 age group will constitute about 15 percent of our population. Clearly, we are aging, and the percentage of old people will continue to increase. This is one reason why there is now so much interest in the field of aging, or gerontology.

LONG AND SHORT LIFE

Some of us will have long lives and some of us will have short lives, with heredity, environment, and luck all playing important roles.

Heredity

Biologists like to joke that, "If you want to live long, choose long-lived parents." While the available data can be interpreted in more than one way, there does seem to be some truth to this. The most compelling argument comes from a comparison of different kinds of animals. For example, rats live about two or three years, while fin whales may live several hundred years. Most other groups, such as the chimpanzees, which live between 15 and 30 years, fall between these extremes. Genes make the difference.

It is probable that genes also make the difference in the respective life spans of men and women. Women outlive men by about five to seven years. Among people under 25 years of age, there are slightly more men than women. In the middle years, there are slightly more women than men; by age 65 to 74 there are about 125 women to every 100 men. After age 75, the ratio is 155 women to 100 men.

It is tempting to think that the fact that women live longer is due to a difference in the lifestyles of men and women, but research on animals suggests otherwise. In most, but not all, animals studied, the female outlived the male; for example, this is true in rats, black widow spiders, mealworms, fruitflies, houseflies, and others. Although this does not prove that women outlive men because of a different biological makeup, it certainly suggests it. Women live longer than men and tend to marry men older than they are—one reason why women are more often widowed than men. Most old men are married but most old women are not.

The biologists' joke about the connection between long life and long-lived parents is based on findings such as the above and on some previous studies which show that long-lived parents have long-lived children. Moreover, a longevity relation among brothers has also been noted; that is, the difference in life span between one brother and another is smaller than the difference between one brother and a stranger.

Environment

While genes may play a role in parent-child and brother-brother life expectancies, nongenetic factors also may be involved. Favorable cultural traits may run in a family. The children of the wealthy not only have more money, but they also tend to be healthier than the children of the poor. A higher economic status results in better nutrition, better housing, and better sanitation, all of which makes for a longer life. In addition, a higher income level is often associated with higher educational levels and with higher status occupations—two conditions that favor longevity.

Keeping Fit

Probably the three most important things we can do to remain healthy and live long are to (1) eat properly, (2) exercise, and (3) refrain from smoking cigarettes. As adults age, more than ever before, fat becomes a killer. Obesity is a road to heart attack. Hardening of the arteries, or arteriosclerosis, is a problem of old age. Blood vessels become rigid and can get clogged, or eventually burst. The walls of these rigid vessels are often lined with a substance called cholesterol, a type of fat which narrows the vessels and blocks them. Fat people tend to eat foods high in cholesterol, such as eggs and beef. These and other types of fats should be avoided in later life. Sugars, carbohydrates, and alcohol should be minimized in the diet.

Few studies investigating health and longevity fail to mention activity and exercise as crucial determinants. In one study, exercise turned out to be the most important factor in longevity. Heart disease is more likely to occur in sedentary people, particularly men.

Hardly anyone today will deny that cigarette smoking influences health and longevity. While smoking used to be connected with only one disease, cancer, there is little doubt now that cigarette smoking is the cause of a variety of health problems and several different kinds of chronic diseases. Smoking by pregnant women can result in smaller babies, abortions, and stillbirths.

Diet, exercise, and no smoking—these are the keys to a healthier and a longer life.

Luck

It was said that heredity, environment, and luck play roles in longevity. Where does luck come in? Luck is success in not being killed in wars or in accidents or in not contracting debilitating diseases. Luck is having the means to ward off economic disaster.

WHO ARE THE OLD?

We are aging; we are extending our life expectancy through medical advances and knowledge of how to keep fit. Individually, we are living longer, and collectively we are becoming old.

Individual Differences

Who are the old? The elderly are not easy to categorize because they are as varied as the members of any other age group or even more so. It is important to keep in mind that most behavioral and physiological measurements which have been made in the laboratory show that there are greater individual differences among the old than among the young, who, we know, are very different individually. The reason the old are more varied than the young is that we first start with the large individual differences of young age. Then, as people grow old, some traits remain the same in what is observed, some get worse, and some get better.

Because of this large variation among older adults most of what can be said about them are generalizations. The situation is not unlike that of the actuarial tables of life insurance companies where the companies bet on people and events and almost always win. We like to think that as individuals we can outlive and outperform the expected average, but do not want to arrange our lives betting heavily that we will win.

There is no one age at which we can say that a person crosses from youth to old age; the transition is gradual. Is being 55 old? Is 75? The psychologist B.L. Neugarten suggested that older adults are best thought of in at least two groupings; that is, the young-old, ranging from 55 to 75, and the old-old, comprising people over 75. Since these two groups are very different —the young-old are healthier than the old-old, their abilities are greater, and the ratio of men to women in this group is greater than in the old-old group—it would seem that more than two groupings could be even more helpful: the young-old (55-65), middle-old (66-77), and old-old (75 and over). Further, in the over-75 category it would be well to make another distinction: the old-old (75 to 84) are different from the very old (85 and over group). The more numerous and differentiated the groupings, the more we can learn about aging and the individual.

General Characteristics

Income. There are many old people who are well-to-do, even rich, but by and large the old are poor, which is one of the reasons why old age is so difficult for them. Ninety percent of older adults have some kind of retirement income, largely from Social Security benefits (see Chapter 4), but often they have not much more than that. In 1975, half of the families with heads of household aged 65 or over had incomes of about $8,000 a year or less. The median income of young families was about $15,000. Half the elderly living alone or with nonrelatives had incomes of less than $2,000 a year!

Health and Disease. Medical advances have largely taken care of acute diseases but little progress has been made regarding the control of chronic diseases. Acute diseases are often intense, but they are short in duration; they frequently result from some kind of infection. Chronic diseases, on the other hand, are long lasting; there might be some slight improvement, but then the condition gets worse again. The cause of these chronic diseases is often not known. People with chronic diseases usually cannot be cured, but they can be helped by being made more comfortable. Many older people suffer from chronic diseases, and the medical bills associated with these conditions are high and often continuous. Those over 65 have medical expenditures three and a half times those of people under 65. Although some help is available from government programs, it hardly ever seems enough. The magnitude of chronic disease expenses for the aged becomes clear when one considers that, although only ten percent of the population is over 65, this segment accounts for 52 percent of the money paid for health care by the government.

The major killers are diseases of the heart, then cancer, and next, cerebrovascular problems (blood vessels in the brain), such as strokes caused by bursting or clogging of vessels. Together, these three conditions account for 70 percent of the deaths of people aged 45 and over. The over-65 age group suffers much more from these diseases than do persons aged 45 to 64.

There are other diseases which are not killers, arthritis for example, but which are painful and disabling. While such diseases, together with the killer diseases, are associated with aging, it is crucial to remember that most older people are not chronically sick or disabled. It has been estimated that approximately 80 percent of older adults are neither physically incapacitated nor in great jeopardy in terms of life and death. In other words, 80 percent are in reasonably good health. For a happy old age, good health is basic.

Residence. It may come as a surprise to many that only about four to five percent of persons over 65 live in institutions. Most of the elderly live with families, usually in their own households, although there is an increasing trend of the elderly to move away from their children. About 28 percent of the 65-plus group lives alone or with nonrelatives. Of those over 85, 17 percent are institutionalized, reflecting an increasing loss of independence with increasing age.

Over the years, many older people have moved to Florida, making this state have the largest percentage of aged residents. States such as Iowa, Nebraska, and Arkansas have experienced an emigration of younger people to other states, which has left much of the older population behind. Despite these population shifts, however, most of the older Americans can be found in the larger states such as California, New York, and Pennsylvania. These states contain the population centers in which one fourth of all older Americans live.

Speaking generally, most young people live in the suburbs, while most old people live in the central city. Overall, then, the typical older person is found in the inner city of a populous state, living in his own home.

REFERENCES

Botwinick, J. *Aging and Behavior*, 2nd ed. Springer Publishing Co., New York, 1978. Chapters 1 and 2.

Hayflick, L. "The Biology of Aging." Master lecture of the series on the Psychology of Aging, 86th Annual Convention of the American Psychological Association, 1978.

Kastenbaum, R.J. and Candy, S.E. "The 4% Fallacy: A Methodological and Empirical Critique of Extended Care Facility Population Statistics." *International Journal of Aging and Human Development*, 1973, 4, 15-21.

Neugarten, B.L. "The Future and the Young-Old." *The Gerontologist*, 1975, 15, 4-9.

Chapter 2

Social Relations

Newsweek magazine recently ran an interesting and important article regarding family relations in China. The focus was on a 29-year-old telegraph operator, Yang Liche who was about to be married. Yang lived in a tiny three-room apartment in Shanghai; showing it to the reporter, he pointed to one of the rooms and said, that one "'will belong to us. Of course, my mother will move in with us for the rest of her days.'" The writer pointed out that although Shanghai is one of the five largest cities in the world he found only one home for the aged there. Golden Age clubs and other social meeting institutions are not needed there, nor are retirement communities. The writer reported further that "old people in China seem secure, almost serene," compared with old people in the United States. The old in China have close family lives and have the respect of the community.

In the United States, older family members are also taken care of, but not in the same way. Middle-aged family members try hard to keep older parents out of institutions and often make considerable sacrifices to do so. However, the emphasis is on the nuclear family where the lifestyles, aspirations, and independence of the father, mother, and children are the prime concerns. Perhaps this is why as many as 17 percent of those over 85 are institutionalized. If we consider those people who go into institutions but who return to their homes at some time, as many as one in five is estimated to be or to have been institutionalized. The trend is increasing. From 1960 to 1970 the number of institutions for the aged increased more than 100 percent. How different this is from China!

Although 20 percent of very old people are institutionalized at some time, it is well to remember that in the majority of cases, 80 percent, family members, including the old, do live together or nearby. It seems, however, that the quality of this living together is different from that in China.

THE OUTSIDE 20 PERCENT

The institutionalized are outside the mainstream of everyday life. The institution may be within the community, but the residents are outside of it. Institutionalized elderly tend to be the unmarried or widowed, and there are likely to be many more women than men because there are almost twice as many women in institutions than men. People without children who live alone or with nonrelatives are apt to end up in institutions.

Most of the outside 20 percent reside in nursing homes and hospitals and tend to be the frail and sick. Hospitalizations occur mostly because of chronic disease and mental problems. Hospitalization in mental hospitals has been declining, but much of the decline has taken place because nursing homes have taken up the slack. Since 1967, more of the mentally ill have been in nursing homes than in all other types of psychiatric facilities.

Family Care

The comparison with China is unfair in some ways, because Americans on the whole try to keep their aged parents from being institutionalized. Older adults are institutionalized mainly when there is little support for them in the community. People who have never married, have no children, or have few or no children nearby are most likely to end up in institutions. Older parents who fight with their middle-aged children present severe problems, but even here the parent does not always end up in an institution. When there is continuous fighting, it is often better for the older person to be in an institution than at home. Institutionalization of an old parent is not synonymous with uncaring. Most frequently, old people are institutionalized when their health has deteriorated.

Families often need help in dealing with their feelings about institutionalizing a parent. Many people feel severe guilt and suffer greatly in caring for their deteriorated parent before committing him or her to an institution. Once they do, they have a feeling of having failed the parent as a son or daughter and of abandoning him. They behave as though institutionalization was death. Visits to the old parent may stop because guilt and grief make the whole experience too painful.

The psychiatrist Butler and his social worker associate Lewis believe that when institutionalizing a parent, there should be an expectation of return and not of final commitment. The institutionalized older person should be kept inside of society, not outside. As a matter of fact, the older person should not be deposited in the institution without preparation; some effort should be made to acquaint the elderly with the institution, and family members might do well to become part of the intake procedures. Families should be advised that there is much that they can do to help and to avoid cutting emotional ties. Institutionalization is not death; it is not the final goodbye. Families can visit and they can take the institutionalized adult on outings; they can also get to know the institution's staff, which could work to the institutionalized member's advantage. Most important, perhaps, families can have the same responsive attitude they have had before.

Types of Homes

Homes for the elderly are either nonprofit or profit-making institutions. Nonprofit homes usually have a religious affiliation. Homes used to be mainly nonprofit until a few years ago, when profit-making became possible with the help of government financing through Medicare and Medicaid programs. As a result, profit-making institutions have greatly increased.

It is true that some nursing homes are bad. Newspapers and magazines have carried investigations exposing some of the more corrupt institutions. The investigations have also uncovered horrors, which should not be taken to mean that most homes are bad (they are not), but merely that investigations are in order. The high cost of nursing homes is a major problem. Medicare payments do not always cover the costs, and this is one reason for the poor quality of many homes.

To make a good selection, long before the day of institutionalization arrives it is advisable to visit homes. This should be done even if the choice is only among good homes. It is best to visit on an ordinary day, without an announcement—look at the kitchens, bedrooms, and lounges, and speak to the staff and residents.

The Very Impaired. Residents suffering mental disorganization or severe physical impairment require close custodial attention, as well as opportunities for mental and physical stimulation. Such residents are often incontinent and cannot feed themselves. Unfortunately, few homes have the staff and resources to meet the needs of such residents.

A series of relocation studies have been conducted. These studies show that for old people in very poor shape the process of institutionalization and adjustment is truly stressful—so much so, in fact, that an appreciable number of them die within the first year of entry. Even moving people involuntarily from one nursing home to another seems to make for this kind of stress. This does not apply to old people in good health moving voluntarily—only to those who are impaired and moving involuntarily.

Persons who are very impaired, mentally or physically, and deteriorating, are not always accepted for admission. Waiting periods are long, and those waiting for admission are often left without help.

Old People With Little or No Deterioration. Deterioration

and severe physical impairment is not a state that is reached by most old people, fortunately. Most old people do not require such close custodial attention; they can take care of themselves, although they require some attention. They may experience some mental confusion, but in the main, they require little care. They do require an active leisure time program. They enjoy attention; they need friends and therefore socialize with one another. They can still enjoy life.

The More Intact. There are also facilities for people who have hardly any disabilities. These facilities go by various names, such as Life Care Facility or Self-Care Units. They are typified by living arrangements which are as close to apartment living as possible, while providing maid service, laundry service, and bus or other transportation service. These residences are for people who find living independently too hard, but who can manage well in surroundings where services and attendants are readily available. Often, only the wife or husband is in need of such a residence, but both enter it to make life easier. Apartments are frequently above a main floor of recreational facilities, which, in turn, are near a general infirmary. It is the more affluent who can pay for such accommodations. The best of such residences provide the intellectual and sensory stimulation required to sustain an active mind.

The next step in independent living is congregate housing, which often resembles apartment houses or garden apartments, but which provides its residents with social services and has a medical staff on hand. It is almost like living independently, but not quite.

THE INSIDE 80 PERCENT

Most older peole are not institutionalized and do not live outside the community life. As previously indicated, only four to five percent of those over 65 live in institutions and 95 to 96 percent live in the community. Put another way, over 90 percent of people over 75 live in the community and 80 percent of those over 85 will never be institutionalized. Mr. Average Old Person lives with or near the family.

Housing

Most older people do not live alone, but among those who do, there are more women than men. Many older people—men and women alike—live with families of adult children or other relatives. The recent, noticeable decline in such arrangements could mean that more and more of the 80 percent of the elderly who generally live inside the community will be living outside of it, in social isolation, even though they are not institutionalized.

Elderly couples who own their homes tend to be better off than those living alone. This is not surprising, perhaps, but older adults heading a household of many younger people tend to be worse off. On the whole, old people in rural areas have poorer housing conditions than those in urban centers, if they own their home.

The psychologist Carp has shown in one of her studies that one in every five elderly people live in substandard housing, for example, without basic plumbing facilities. The elderly living in these homes usually lack the money to make the necessary repairs. They suffer, as do people of all ages, from inflation and rising prices, but the older person must often cope with this on a fixed income. Many older people do not complain and may seem comfortable in their broken down homes. Some researchers believe that as a group older people just do not complain; everyone thinks they are content but really they are not.

Of course, not all old people live in their own houses. Many live in apartments, but these also tend to be in old, poor buildings. About 600,000 old people, men in particular, reside in old city hotels and boarding houses, which are often dilapidated and, from the perspective of most people, in miserable condition. Residents might be found watching TV and hardly noticing one another. Such unfortunate people are hardly part of the inside 80 percent. Many of these accommodations are in high crime areas and the inhabitants are easy targets for muggings and other abuse.

Older people with more money are apt to have better housing. Many of the elderly in the lower middle class, though, have taken to living in mobile homes which seems to be working well, giving them a sense of community and security. For the wealthy among the aged, there are luxury retirement communities, as well as some that are not so luxurious. But for most of the elderly, housing presents an increasingly difficult problem.

Family

There has been a pattern of family life in this country, from the time following the Great Depression. This pattern, however, appears headed for change.

Up to Now. The family pattern to the 1980s has been for young adult children to leave home and set themselves up on their own. The children move away and leave the aging parents with what has come to be known as the *empty nest.* The children are no longer part of the nuclear family. Some parents feel almost lost with their children gone, others feel free and may even experience a second honeymoon. One study, disclosing positive feelings when the last child had left home, concluded that it might be more appropriate to call such a home the *child-free home* instead of the empty nest.

Typically, it is the mother more than the father who has these positive or negative emotions. After all, it is the mother who has tended to the children and maintained the home while the father spent much of his time at work. This mother-father division of labor seems to be changing; it appears that in the future the father will experience more of the empty nest emotions than the mother.

By the time the father retires from work, adjustments to the empty nest have usually been made. One of the more important family patterns involves the frequent contacts between aging parents and their adult offspring and with the children of their offspring. As can be expected, the closer in distance the two parties live, the greater the frequency of the contacts. Most old people have close relationships with their families and consider nearness of the family crucial. In fact, older people tend to see more of distant relatives who live nearby than of sons and daughters that live further away. Frequent contacts with relatives seems more typical of older people of higher socioeconomic status than of those in less fortunate circumstances.

Generally speaking, older people prefer not to live with their children, but circumstances sometimes dictate differently. Sickness, money difficulties, or widowhood often make it necessary for the elderly to remain with their children. Failing this, older people like to visit relatives and to be visited by them. They remain inside society by contact with their extended families.

Different From Now On? An interesting article appeared in the St. Louis *Post-Dispatch* not very long ago. It referred to an economist, Allvine, who is on the faculty of Georgia Institute of Technology. He believes that the changing economy—energy shortages, inflation, high housing costs, uncertain economic times—is making it difficult for young people to leave home. Young people, Mr. Allvine was quoted as saying, are becoming more and more dependent on their aging parents. "The empty nest," he concluded, "may not be so empty anymore...there is more of a hanging on...the American family is going to have to stick together more than it has in the past to survive economically."

Sons and daughters graduating from colleges are not getting sufficiently high-paying jobs to allow them to leave home and support themselves. Some families, Allvine said, are even converting their homes and garages to accommodate the return of their young adult children. No longer, he said, are the young buying cars, renting apartments, or buying houses. Furthermore, many young people cannot afford to live in the neighborhoods of their parents. "Three generations have enjoyed increasingly better life styles," the article said, "the young generation is going to live a toned-down life style."

If this is coming to pass, the empty nest will become a thing of the past, and family visits will change to more intense family interactions. It remains to be seen whether such a change will strengthen or weaken American family relationships.

A More Radical Change

Another change is foreseen, one very much more important than the return to the empty nest. This change is so revolutionary as to threaten American family life as we know it. Radical adjustments will be necessary, not only for the elderly, but for people of all ages.

This was indicated by Masnick, a sociologist, and Bane, an educator, in a study entitled, "The Nation's Families: 1960-1990" (1980). It is predicted that the nuclear family of a husband, wife, and young children is on the way out for the majority of people. In 1960, 55 percent of American households consisted of the nuclear family with children under 15. By the end of the 1880s, this will be true for less than a third of the households. There are several reasons for this. First, there is a declining marriage rate. By 1990 between one third and one half of women aged 20 to 29 will never have married. Further, the number of children born to a couple is declining. Also, more and more couples are divorcing. Of the 20 million new households expected to be established between 1975 to 1990, it is predicted that only three to four million will be married couples. The remaining households will be headed by adults who never married or who are divorced or widowed.

The vast majority of households in 1990 will see the parents in the labor force. This trend is already occurring. If there is one parent, he or she will be working. If there are two parents, both will be working. Adjustments of many kinds will have to be made. Who will care for the children at home? Who will provide the necessary emotional and physical support of elderly members of the extended family?

Friendships

Fortunately, most old people have friends as well as family. They tend to have old friends—old in years and old in standing. Old friends are therefore often the best friends. Besides, old people often feel unwanted by the young. As the psychologist Kalish said, "Perhaps they feel more at home with people who have shared their...memories...of the same ballplayers, movie actors, automobiles, politicians, dances...slang...clothing styles." People of all ages need friends as well as relatives. Friends are supports, especially in difficult times.

Not all friends of the elderly, however, are old friends. A substantial percentage of older people has been reported to have formed close friendships within the previous year or so. Not all friends need to be close; neighbors and casual acquaintances also make for a pleasant day.

How do older people meet friends? Much like anyone else. It is easier, of course, to make friends in a place where many people congregate. Most professionals frown on age segregation. Instead, they are in favor of the elderly living in places where people of all ages are to be found. One study, however, suggested otherwise. A sociologist by the name of Rosow examined a large number of apartment buildings in Cleveland and found that most friendships between older people developed in buildings which had a high percentage of older people. Most of the friendships were made between people of similar age. These new friends were seen as more important and closer than old friends not immediately at hand.

Widowhood

Despite all the changes of the last decade, marriage and having children is still considered "in" among most people and certainly among most older people. For older people, however, the death of a spouse is a very realistic fear, and one that women are more justified to have. The sociologist Ward phrased it well:

"The new widow can no longer play the role of confidant, lover, housekeeper, or 'member of a couple'". . . . As Ward indicated, widowed people lose the opportunity to have three things we all want and need: the feeling to belong and share; love and attachment; the need to be valued, to feel competent and responsible. A good marriage fulfills these needs; the loss of a spouse usually leaves some of them unmet.

The extended family can be of great help when there is a loss of a spouse, but the help is not always enough. The death of a spouse causes disruption, depression, and, in turn, even death. But most people recover from the disruption and depression. Some, especially those whose spouses were sick and disabled for many years, seem to be in better spirits than before; there is a new independence, a new outlook on life, and a new opportunity. There are, however, problems, often concerning money. There are other changes, too—friends do not extend invitations as frequently because the widowed is a single. In addition, people are uncomfortable with those who grieve. Adult children become particularly important at this time, especially daughters who tend to be closer and more attentive than sons. With health and money, recovery from grief is apt to be more likely and quicker.

Those living alone obviously tend to be lonely, but loneliness is not synonymous with aloneness. Some people prefer being alone; others get used to it. Loneliness comes from not having anyone to be with and talk with. Widowed people and others living alone can find social sustenance if someone close by becomes a confidant. Three things are important at all ages for contentment, particularly in later life. One was indicated in the previous chapter, i.e., health; income and having a friend are the other two.

ATTITUDES TOWARD THE AGED

By and large, young people have a negative view of the aged. Unfortunately, so do the aged themselves. People stereotype the aged; they say negative things about them and expect negative things of them. Literature, television, and jokes put old people down; society does not value the roles that old people play. Old age, furthermore, is associated with poor health, low income, and closeness to death. People are uncomfortable with these stages of life.

Life cannot be pleasant if one is surrounded by negative attitudes. Fortunately, a relatively recent study suggests that things may be changing. A questionnaire disclosed that older people rated their lives as better than younger people did when they projected themselves into the future as older adults. The best years were seen to increase with the age of the person answering the questions. Old age need not be bad. It can be a period of relaxation, fulfillment, and satisfaction of having done all that had to be done, of having done what was expected of one. There is pleasure on looking back and seeing that personal interests and wants were met.

REFERENCES

Butler, R.N. and Lewis, M.I. *Aging and Mental Health*. The C.V. Mosby Co., St. Louis, Mo., 1977. Chapter 11.

Carp, F.M. "Housing and Living Arrangements of Older People." In *Handbook of Aging and the Social Sciences*, edited by R.H. Binstock and E. Shanas. Van Nostrand Reinhold Co., New York, 1976.

Gwirtzman, M. "Restored Treasure." *Newsweek*, Sept. 10, 1979, p. 15.

Kalish, R.A. *Late Adulthood: Perspectives on Human Development*. Brooks/ Cole Publishing Co., Monterey, Ca., 1975. Chapters 4 and 5.

Lowenthal, M.F. "Social Networks and Isolation." *Handbook of Aging and Social Sciences*, edited by R.H. Binstock and E. Shanas. Van Nostrand Reinhold Co., New York, 1976.

Masnick, G. and Bane, M.J. "The Nation's Families: 1960-1990," Joint Center for Urban Studies of M.I.T. and Harvard universities, Cambridge, Mass., 1980.

Palmore, E., Cleveland, W.P., Nowlin, J.B., Ramm, D. and Siegler, I. "Stress and Adaptation in Later Life." *Journal of Gerontology*, 1979, 34, 841-851.

Rosow, I. *Social Integration of the Aged*. Free Press, New York, 1967.

St. Louis *Post-Dispatch*, news article, Dec. 26, 1979.

Ward, R.A. *The Aging Experience*. J.B. Lippincott Co., New York, 1979. Chapters 2, 8, 9, 11.

Chapter 3

The Closeness of Family

Older people suffer real hardships due to loss and inability, but fortunately this is the fate of only a minority of the aged. The majority has more pleasant lives. Of course there are problems unique to their age groups and stations in life, but this is true of all people.

Severe, disabling problems are rarely present until people reach their sixties. In their seventies, more of the aged need help, but it is not until the eighties that the need for support, emotional and otherwise, becomes pronounced. During the late eighties, the person who is independent and in control of his or her destiny is the exception. Serious problems demand help. In a vast majority of cases, the most concerned are family members.

When problems present themselves, it is the middle-aged children to whom the elderly look for help. This help is sometimes given willingly, sometimes not, but in most cases the children are there when needed. They are there over and beyond the assistance provided by institutional bureaucracies.

This chapter deals with the role the middle-aged child plays in the life of an aged parent.

MIDDLE-AGED SONS AND DAUGHTERS

Social Myth

As we saw in the previous chapter, family concern for the aged parent is the rule, not the exception. The emotional tie between children and parents is often the major "support system." Although the emphasis in the United States is on the nuclear family, we do take care of our older parents. In fact, the idea that the elderly are left destitute, that there is no emotional closeness between middle-aged children and their parents, has been labeled a social myth. Perhaps more than anyone else, it was the sociologist Shanas who investigated a large number of family arrangements and disclosed this myth in contemporary American society. Older people are not alienated from their children. The fact that middle-aged children live apart from their old parents does not mean that the latter are neglected. Half of the old people who live alone have children within a 10 minute distance. Among the elderly who have children, and more than three quarters do, if one child lives far away, one or more of the children are apt to live close by and to see the old parent often. In addition, the old person sees brothers and sisters; so, it is clear, most people are not left alone, despite the pattern of the nuclear family.

From the point of view of the elderly, the emotional ties with their children are most important. Even if they break off some social contacts, the aged do not separate themselves from their children, regardless of how unsatisfying that relationship is. There are exceptions, of course, but on the whole, family ties override even pain in interaction.

This is the general picture. However, not everyone accepts this. Peterson, another sociologist, studied old people moving into a middle-class retirement community. In contrast to Shanas, he found that close to 50 percent had no close living relatives, and he came to the conclusion that "a great mythology surrounds the wish of the older person to associate with children and grandchildren. One sentimental view is that intergeneration contacts are essential to the life satisfaction of older persons." Peterson rejects this "sentimental view," indicating that the older person values independence and prefers it to intrusion by family. Perhaps the fact that he studied people moving into a retirement community colored Peterson's perceptions, which seem at variance with the general picture of closeness between an old parent and a middle-aged son or daughter.

While closeness involves help, the help is not always a one-way street. A study on low-income urban people showed that over three quarters of the elderly reported helping their children in some way—usually by giving gifts. But about 80 percent of the elderly received help from their children in return. Although this study was concerned with low-income, urban adults, there is no reason to think results would be different with other social classes.

The relationship of mutual help between children and parents is of necessity long term. Parents become older and widowed. Contrary to some opinion, late-life remarriages are the exception rather than the rule. There is a scarcity of older single men; also, courtship depends on health, income, and mobility. The old parent is in need of children's help for a long period of time.

Independence

Older adults value their independence; they want to be able to make their own decisions. There is no disagreement on this point, nor on the fact that intrusion by children and grandchildren is resented, as Peterson suggested. Most everyone prizes independence and just about everyone wants to be able to take care of his own money and household and to manage his own affairs—the old are no exception. Older people want this independence, but they also want to have close and frequent relations with their adult children and their grandchildren, even though they prefer not to live with them. Independence, however, often becomes progressively more difficult for the older person to retain; self-reliance and self-direction are possible only when health and wealth permit it. Aging frequently means a progressive loss of independence because of diminishing ability to function alone. The dependent person feels miserable.

The desire for independence and for the ability to stay at home, rather than in an institution, are often intertwined. This is where middle-aged sons and daughters can make their contribution. They can make it possible for the aged parent to stay at home longer. Being able to stay at home enhances feelings of self-worth.

Role Reversals

As the middle-aged child helps more and more, he assumes a more dominant position in the lives of older parents. An interesting pattern of role reversal evolves, which intensifies the longer people live. The middle-aged child or the grandchild has responsibilities regarding the old parent that are different from those of years back. Frequently, these responsibilities reverse former roles. There is a switch in the independent-dependent relationship, with the parent becoming the more dependent.

Disabilities such as failing eyesight and hearing, arthritis, and poor memory make the old person more vulnerable and in need of more attention than before. Assistance is required from a child or grandchild, and depending on the extent of that assistance, the elderly's dependency increases. Dependency, however, used to be the child's role, not the parent's.

The clinical psychologist Schwartz prefers to think of this change in role relations as a switch to mutual dependence on the part of both parent and child rather than as a switch from independence to dependence. He reasons that the child is dependent on the parent from birth. Even as the child strives, and succeeds in attaining physical independence, some psychological dependence remains at least until the time of the parent's death. The younger person now ministering to the older parent therefore creates a balance of mutual dependence.

The more realistic the old parent is about shifting to mutual dependence, the better he or she will respond to the son or daughter as a helping adult and not as a child. The more realistic the son or daughter is about shifting to mutual dependence, the easier it is to perceive of the increasing physical dependency of the aging parent as mutual dependency and not as a regression into second childhood. This kind of relationship will lead to a peer-like friend relationship. Mutual dependency is not to be avoided; on the contrary, it should become the goal.

Help or Intrusion

A feeling of mutual dependency maximizes the opportunity for the son or daughter to help the parent and minimizes the chances of intrusion into the privacy and independence of the parent. A problem for well-meaning sons and daughters who are emotionally close to their parents is when to stop helping, because the intended help is perceived as being overly solicitous and dominating. Love can be overbearing.

Silverstone and Hyman in their book *You and Your Aging Parent* have discussed this point in great detail. Middle-aged children can hover over their parents and overpower them. They can spend too much time with them and encourage complete dependence before it is ever necessary. Middle-aged children may do this because of guilt feelings, or because they may still be emotionally dependent on the parents and fear their loss. Focusing their attention on the aged parent gives the children a feeling of protecting the parents and thus keeping them so that they, the children, will not be left parentless.

Silverstone and Hyman have also noted that the opposite can happen: sometimes the son or daughter feels that care should be given but does not provide it. Guilt might set in, but rather than blame themselves, the children may blame someone else—the nursing home is at fault or the other family members should do more. This technique, often unconscious, may divert blame from themselves, but the other family members usually do not react kindly to it; they become angry, seek to place the blame where it correctly belongs, and family fights start.

It is important for the middle-aged son or daughter to recognize that both too much and too little concern can have a negative effect. The right amount of help is often difficult to offer but can more nearly be achieved when both parent and child have a realistic understanding of what needs to be done and what feelings underlie the mutual relationships.

Double Bind

People speak to each other and yet do not understand each other—they fail to communicate. Worse still, people speak to each other and convey mixed signals; they interact on different levels, sometimes saying one thing on one level but conveying something else on another. This requires some sort of answer which often is equally contradictory. For example, a mother finds her teenage daughter doing something that she has been forbidden to do and tells her that she will not "tell daddy because it will hurt him." Later in the conversation, the mother says, "I don't withhold anything from your father because I don't want him to keep anything from me. Besides, it's wrong to do it." The daughter, on her part, must reconcile the two messages her mother is conveying. This double bind might lead her to answer, "Why don't you leave me alone," which takes care of nothing.

Herr and Weakland provide a much more subtle example of a double bind involving an 80-year-old woman who unexpectedly became widowed. She seemed frightened, uncertain, and confused. She was very much aggrieved. She became more involved with her children, but her children gave her contradictory messages—the double bind. They told her that they would help her to remain independent, but if she refused their help, this would only show that she was not capable of independence. In other words, the 80-year-old mother either takes orders from her children and thus loses her independence, or she does not take them, thus seemingly admitting that she cannot take care of herself anymore. Soon, whatever she does is no good and shows that she cannot take care of herself. After a while she begins to believe it.

Recognizing the possibility of a double bind is the first step in avoiding it. The second step is much harder. If we can understand and recognize our own feelings and motives, we can more nearly speak on one level without contradiction.

The Hardest Decision

After all efforts (be they helpful or intrusive) to help the aging parent have been exhausted, after recognizing the independency-dependency needs and responding to them or failing to do so, after eliminating the double bind problem or trying to, and after having done all that is possible for the middle-aged child to do, a point may be reached where life for everyone is too painful to proceed without institutionalization. Typically, when the disabled person lives with a spouse, it is the spouse who has the hard, painful job of helping the disabled member. The spouse also has to make the painful decision regarding institutionalization. This decision is often made with the help of the middle-aged children, but not always. When there is no surviving spouse, the decision is up to the middle-aged son or daughter.

The Sick Older Person. The disabled person may be housebound because of physical impairment or mental deterioration; he or she may have to spend time in bed, may be incontinent, or may have little or no memory left. As mentioned before, if there is a spouse, he or she is the major caretaker. In fact, men often take over the traditionally female role of caretaker when necessary, and "women find strength to turn and lift bedfast husbands." In such cases, the extended family (middle-aged children, brothers, and sisters) helps mainly by moral support, visiting, and keeping the elderly parents feeling wanted. Old people first turn to their spouses, then to their children, next neighbors, and, if all else fails, to bureaucratic replacements such as social workers, ministers, and community agencies.

Elderly wives caring for disabled husbands have special problems. They are often under a great amount of stress, feel depressed, lonely, isolated, and overworked. In such situations, the help from middle-aged sons and daughters is especially appreciated.

If the disabilities and accompanying needs for custodial care are prolonged and get progressively worse, stress and conflict become a part of the lives of the helping middle-aged children as well as of the helping spouse. When there is no surviving spouse the pressure on the middle-aged adult is more severe.

A point is reached where institutionalization is unavoidable. People tend to think of institutionalization as a complete severance from their loved ones. This is not so. An important series of interviews was carried out with both institutionalized parents and their middle-aged children in which "the majority of people of both generations expressed an improvement of or continuation of close family ties following institutionalization." It is clear, then, that institutional care often reduces stress and conflict and enhances family relations.

The Decision Point. When does one reach the point of having to decide on institutionalization? How do we know the time has arrived? How are guilt feelings handled in "institutionalizing *my* mother or father?" Answers to these questions are difficult. Although the decision to institutionalize an aging parent is among the most unpleasant ones for the middle-aged son or daughter to make, it should be made before the stress of caretaking becomes overpowering, but not before every effort has been made to see if the disabled parent can be recovered.

As indicated in the previous chapter, middle-aged children and the healthier parent often need help in dealing with their feelings about institutionalizing the loved one. No one likes the idea of it. The decision involves guilt and suffering. To maximize the positive aspects of institutionalization, family ties should be kept strong, including frequent contacts between the institutionalized person and the rest of the family. The older person should not be "deposited" in the institution without having been carefully prepared, if he or she is capable of understanding.

GRANDCHILDREN

Middle-aged children often think that their own children are a source of extreme pleasure to their aging parents. This usually is the case, but not always. There are times when the older parent resents being considered a baby-sitter or being asked to perform other household responsibilities. Grandparents have lives of their own.

Contrary to the stereotype of the old grandparent, most people become grandparents when they are still in their forties. Few people have new grandchildren after their mid-sixties. Great-grandparenthood is becoming ever more common. Currently, about 40 percent of older people in the United States are great-grandparents. It is not so rare to find a very old parent living in the same household as an old child, or living nearby. The mother may be 95, the son 75. Both mother and son may need help from the grandchild, aged 55.

How Do Grandparents
Respond to Grandchildren?

Most grandparents enjoy grandparenting. A study of grandparents in their fifties and sixties found that most took pleasure in being with their grandchildren. However, as many as one in three expressed some disappointment.

Not all people approach grandparenting in the same way; the study identified five different types of grandparents, of which three were what we usually think of when we say "grandparent." One group liked to bestow favors on the grandchildren but to leave the main responsibility to the parents. Another group liked to take over the parents' job, but only when invited to do so; this was more true of women than men. A third group, primarily men, liked to be the source of wisdom or skills. A fourth group was quite different from the others. It consisted of people who joined the children in activities and had fun with them; they did not bother being adult authority figures. The last group did not fit the traditional concept of grandparents; they showed up only rarely to see their grandchildren, and then mainly on special occasions. Their contact with their grandchildren was fleeting and superficial.

How Do Grandchildren Respond to Grandparents?

As may be expected, young children respond differently to grandparents than do older children. A study by Kahana and Kahana showed that children aged four or five responded to grandparents according to what they got—food, presents, and love. There was little interpersonal give and take in an emotional sense other than the enjoyment of being with the family and getting presents. Older children, about eight or nine, were found to interact more with their grandparents; they went to ball games with them, played cards, and did things together. These children looked up to their grandparents.

As the children moved closer to the teenager stage, say at age 11 or 12, they started to withdraw from the grandparents. There is not much of a grandparent-grandchild relationship left once the latter has become a teenager. However, a study by Robertson disclosed that as teenagers grow into young adulthood, there is still much feeling left. They do not see their grandparents as old-fashioned or out of touch but consider them an important source of influence. They even feel responsibility toward their grandparents. Adult grandchildren, like adult children, provide the older grandparent with emotional support and, at times, with tangible help.

Life is a two-way street; family members of all ages experience mutual dependence and independence, even if their love is not always without conflict.

REFERENCES

Atchley, R.C. *The Social Forces in Later Life.* Wadsworth Publishing Co., Belmont, Ca., 1972. Chapters 11 and 18.

Brown, A.S. "Satisfying Relationships for the Elderly and Their Patterns of Disengagement." *Gerontologist,* 1974, 14, 258-262.

Cantor, M.H. "Life Space and Social Support System of the Inner City Elderly of New York." *Gerontologist,* 1975, 15, 23-27.

Fengler, A.P. and Goodrich, N. "Wives of Elderly Disabled Men: the Hidden Patients." *Gerontologist,* 1979, 19, 175-183.

Herr, J.J. and Weakland, J.H. "Communications Within Family Systems: Growing Older Within and With the Double Bind." *Aging Parents,* edited by P.K. Ragan. The University of Southern California Press, Los Angeles, 1979.

Kahana, B. and Kahana, E. "Grandparenthood from the Perspective of the Developing Grandchild." *Developmental Psychology,* 1970, 3, 98-105.

Neugarten, B.L. and Weinstein, K.K. "The Changing American Grandparent." *Journal of Marriage and the Family,* 1964, 26, 199-204.

Peterson, J.A. "The Relationships of Middle-aged Children and Their Parents." *Aging Parents,* edited by P.K. Ragan. The University of Southern California Press, Los Angeles, 1979.

Robertson, J.F. "Significance of Grandparents: Perceptions of Young Adult Grandchildren." *Gerontologist,* 1976, 16, 137-140.

Robinson, B. and Thurnher, M. "Taking Care of Aged Parents: A Family Cycle Transition." *Gerontologist,* 1976, 19, 586-593.

Schwartz, A.N. "Psychological Dependency: An Emphasis on the Later Years." *Aging Parents,* edited by P.K. Ragan. The University of Southern California Press, Los Angeles, 1979.

Shanas, E. "Social Myth as Hypothesis: The Case of the Family Relations of Old People." *Gerontologist,* 1979, 19, 3-9.

Shanas, E. "The Family as a Social Support System in Old Age." *Gerontologist,* 1979, 19, 169-174.

Silverstone, B. and Hyman, H.K. *You and Your Aging Parent.* Random House, Inc. (Pantheon Books), New York, 1976. Chapters 2 and 5.

Smith, K.F. and Bengtson, V.L. "Positive Consequences of Institutionalization: Solidarity Between Elderly Parents and Their Middle-Aged Children." *Gerontologist,* 1979, 19, 438-447.

Treas, J. and VanHilst, A. "Marriage and Remarriage Rates Among Older Americans." *Gerontologist,* 1976, 16, 132-136.

Chapter 4

Services for the Elderly

by Dorothy Farrar, Ph.D.*

The vast majority of elderly Americans live in private residences, either alone or with family. Most of these people are in the mainstream of community life. At least 80 percent of the elderly lives this way, perhaps more. Chapter 2 referred to them as the inside 80 percent, in contrast to the outside 20 percent, who are institutionalized. Although 80 percent lives inside community life, this does not mean that all of them are without need of some help from the community. In fact, just the opposite is true. In 1975, the U.S. Senate Committee on Aging estimated that about three million older persons in the inside group were in need of some type of assistance to continue staying in their own homes. One way to help these people is through public and private agencies.

Most social service programs are funded at least in part by the federal government. In 1977, *Newsweek* magazine published an article about the graying of America. This article examined the growth of the older population and its impact on American

*Department of Psychology, Washington University. St. Louis, MO. 63130.

society. One of the most visible impacts of this growth was the increase in funding of social services for older adults. In many ways, the federal budget is also graying as programs for older persons receive larger and larger percentages of the federal service dollar. For example, from 1965, when the Older Americans Act was passed, to 1974, government programs under this law increased from $7.5 million to over $130 million. This program and others are directed toward keeping older people content and healthy in the community.

TYPES OF SERVICES

The sociologist Ward lists four types of services geared to keep the elderly in the community: preventive, treatment, protective and support, and referral services.

Preventive services include counseling programs, especially as they relate to medical and dental needs. Hearing and seeing are especially important (see Chapter 10). Treatment services include diagnosis and care of health problems before institutionalization is necessary. Protective services include legal help, consumer education, and home management and repair. In some ways, referral services are the focal service: they tell the older person what is needed, where help can be gotten, and how to go about getting it. Information on transportation, food, medical, and other services needs to be coordinated. Without this kind of help, the older person can be lost; with it, he can be saved and remain part of the inside 80 percent.

The Older Americans Act

The passage of the Older Americans Act in 1965 was a very important event in the development of special programs for older people. This law resulted from years of careful study and planning by many different groups involved with the elderly. The planning process actually started in 1950 when President

Truman called for a national conference to study the problems of older adults. Other conferences were held in 1961 and 1971. These conferences came to be known as the White House Conferences on Aging. The White House Conferences brought researchers and practitioners in the field of gerontology together with other people in the community to discuss the needs of the elderly population. Much of the information obtained from these conferences was incorporated into the law.

One very important aspect of the Older Americans Act is that there are no eligibility requirements other than age. Every person in the United States over the age of 60 can participate in Older Americans Act Programs.

The Act lists the following objectives for all those over 60:

1. an adequate income;
2. the best possible physical and mental health;
3. suitable housing at reasonable cost;
4. full services for those who require institutional care to restore their health;
5. equal employment opportunity;
6. retirement with dignity;
7. a meaningful existence;
8. efficient community services;
9. benefits of knowledge from research; and
10. freedom, independence, and individual initiative in the planning and management of life.

Perhaps the most noteworthy outcome of this law was the creation of a network of agencies to serve older people. The federal government established the Administration on Aging, a federal agency which serves as the administrative and integrative structure for state and local programs and services. Under the Act, each state is required to establish an agency called the Office on Aging. These state agencies plan and coordinate social services for older adults at the local level. Neighborhood senior citizen centers are the local part of the network. These senior citizen centers are important for several reasons. They not only provide the programs authorized by the Act, but also are involved with other programs and funding sources. Their goals are to provide as many programs as possible in one central place, to maximize benefits and services for older adults, and to minimize confusion and red tape.

Another significant change brought about by the Older Americans Act was the development of a network of service resources. Agencies funded through the Act are required to coordinate the various resources. What this means is that each program from the federal level down to the local level works to expand the services to older adults through contact and cooperation with other service programs. Before 1965, there was very little coordination among programs because the administrative structure necessary for this type of planning and coordination did not exist.

Federal laws are broken down into major sections or parts known as titles. Each title outlines a specific project or service. The funding of each law is also broken down by titles, making it possible for Congress to specify how the appropriated money will be spent. The different services of the Older Americans Act are also identified by title. For example, Title III involves social services and nutrition programs; Title IV covers education and training, and so on. Some titles are broken down further by letter; for example III-B and III-C.

Title III-B. The purpose of this section of the Act is to assist state and local agencies to develop comprehensive programs of social services for the elderly. The thrust of these programs is to meet the needs of senior citizens in the major areas of health, housing, transportation, and counseling. The most visible aspect of this program is the network of neighborhood senior citizen centers. These centers provide social settings and recreational programs which alleviate loneliness and social isolation. Many of these centers provide transportation for basic needs, such as grocery shopping, doctors' visits, and trips to other agencies, such as Social Security or Medicare offices.

The senior citizen centers also offer the crucial services of information and referral. When problems arise, specially trained staff members work with older persons or their families to help arrive at solutions and determine sources of assistance. In this way, older persons can be helped even if the needed services are not available at the senior citizen center itself.

Outreach is another important program funded through Title III-B. Often, time comes when an older person may become "lost" in the community. Outreach workers follow up reports about such older persons who need help. Many of the elderly live alone and have no one to lend a helping hand. Outreach workers can provide company, perhaps cheer them up and assess their specific needs. Arrangements can then be made with the proper agencies to deliver the necessary services.

Other projects which have been funded through Title III-B include (1) legal services—where lawyers come into senior citizen centers or nursing homes to assist with legal problems; (2) chore services—where help is provided with housecleaning and simple personal care, such as laundry or grocery shopping; (3) welfare counseling—to ensure that the person is receiving all entitled benefits; and (4) home repair—where workers come to make minor home repairs which, if uncorrected, can endanger the safety or well-being of an older person. Typical repairs include simple plumbing and wiring, or installation of locks and smoke alarms.

Title III-C. Many people consider Title III-C to be the most important part of the Older Americans Act because it is concerned with special meal programs for older adults. The purpose of Title III-C is to provide senior citizens with hot meals which supply them with one third of their daily nutritional requirements. The law further requires that these meals be provided in a pleasant setting.

In many cases the lunch at the senior citizen center is the only complete and balanced meal the older person has—one reason why there are usually waiting lists for meals at senior citizen centers. Even the tremendous increases in funding over the past few years cannot keep up with the increased demand for food.

One good aspect of this program is that the meals can be planned to fit the special needs and interests of the senior citizens attending a particular center; for example, kosher food can be ordered for elderly Jewish people. Meals served in senior citizen centers are referred to as congregate meals.

The home-delivered meals program is an extension of the congregate meals program. For those elderly who are unable to come to the center for their meals, the law also mandates nutritious food. A home-delivered meal can be either a hot meal or a frozen dinner that can be enjoyed at the person's leisure. This program is important for shut-ins who otherwise would suffer from malnutrition. The social contact with those bringing the food is an additional benefit.

Title IV. This section covers a wide range of educational programs for the elderly as well as special research on the social service needs of older people. One part benefits older adults only indirectly and that is the part that pays for the graduate training of people of any age who intend to work in the field of aging. Among the professionals trained in these programs are social workers, psychologists, lawyers, urban planners, and nursing home administrators.

Other Title IV funds are used to help train the people who work in local senior citizen centers. For example, nutrition workers may be given special training in the emotional problems of aging to help them recognize these types of problems in their clients. Or information and referral workers might review Older American Act programs with the staffs of other agencies, such as the United Way, to make sure that people who come into contact with older adults or their families know where to turn for help.

Title IV also includes funding of special courses and programs for older people at local schools and colleges. For example, older adults can enroll at colleges or junior colleges and pay less tuition than others, with the government making up

the difference. Just about anything related to the educational needs of and for the elderly is covered by this section of
the law.

The Older Americans Act covers many other services,
depending on the needs of a particular community, but the
major programs are those under Titles III-B, III-C and IV.

Social Security Act: Title XX

Many people are familiar with the parts of the Social Security Act that provide retirement income and medical help (see
Chapter 6). There is one section of the Social Security Act, however, that is not nearly as well known, called Title XX. In fact, it
was so little known that for several years most states did not use
the funds that were available to them under this law, even though
there were many elderly persons in need of services and eligible
to receive them. The husband and wife team Hendricks and
Hendricks noted that this money had been available since the
mid-1960s but was not widely used for services for older adults
until 1972.

Title XX of the Social Security Act covers many of the same
programs as the Older Americans Act. There are funds for congregate meals, home-delivered meals, transportation, and chore
services. There are also funds for legal services, educational,
and recreational programs; in addition, there are provisions for
geriatric day care and counseling. According to the law, the goal
of Title XX is to provide services enabling people to reach and
maintain the highest possible level of independence and sound
health.

Title XX is what is known as a certification program. In
other words, a person must be certified as eligible to receive
services based on their income. In order to become certified, a
person applies for Title XX through the state welfare department or the department of social services. In many states, social
workers will visit the homes of the elderly if they are homebound

and unable to go to the welfare office to apply. There are two major differences between Title XX and the Older Americans Act. One, the Social Security Act has an income eligibility requirement. While the programs of the Older Americans Act are open to all persons 60 and over, regardless of income, only persons with incomes below certain amounts are eligible under Title XX. Income level requirements vary from state to state, depending on the cost of living and the median income for the area. In addition to economic eligibility, people need to be 60 or older to qualify, unless there is a certified medical disability.

The second difference involves the source of funding. All money for the Older Americans Act comes from the federal government. Under Title XX of the Social Security Act, the federal government provides 75 percent of the money while the state contributes the remaining 25 percent, either in cash or with other services. The federal funds are granted to state departments of welfare or social services. In many places, local senior citizen centers receive Title XX funds directly. Since Older Americans Act money is often not enough to meet all needs, Title XX funds enable the senior citizen centers to help a great number of people with services identical to those available through the Older Americans Act.

ACTION

Another federal program for older people is known as ACTION. ACTION differs from other programs in that it provides volunteers with a chance to do things they enjoy at the same time they are doing a good deed. Two of the best known ACTION programs are VISTA and the Peace Corps, developed for people of all ages. The ACTION programs specially designed for older people are the Retired Senior Volunteer Program, the Foster Grandparents Program, the Senior Companion Program, and the Service Corps of Retired Executives.

Retired Senior Volunteer Program (*RSVP*). Many communities benefit from the services provided by RSVP volunteers. Anyone 60 years of age and older who wants to become involved in useful service to others is encouraged to do so through this project. RSVP volunteers serve in schools, libraries, nursing homes, hospitals, and senior citizen centers. Volunteers are not paid but are reimbursed for transportation and expenses.

Foster Grandparents Program. In this program, low income older persons provide care and attention to disadvantaged children. In most places, foster grandparents work 20 hours a week, sometimes in schools, sometimes in day care centers, sometimes in nursing homes. Their job is to give as much love, understanding, and attention as they can through simple activities and direct contact with children. ACTION often refers to this project as its most successful program because it helps two different groups at one time, older people of low income who need to feel useful and lonely children who desperately need attention. Foster grandparents receive a minimum wage, transportation as needed, and a meal each day they work.

Senior Companion Program (*SCP*). This program is very similar to the Foster Grandparents Program, except that the recipients of this service are older persons instead of children. Low income older adults assist the very old and infirm; they provide friendship, care, and attention. Duties may also include reading, letter writing, simple housekeeping, cooking, or personal hygiene. Senior companions receive a minimum wage, transportation if needed, and a meal each day they work.

Service Corps of Retired Executives (*SCORE*). This program is a joint venture of ACTION and the Small Business Administration. SCORE provides valuable assistance to small business owners and persons needing help in setting up their own business. Retired businessmen and women lend their experience and know-how gained from long years in the working world. These volunteers have helped approximately 200,000 businesses since the program began in 1965.

Housing

There have been many federal laws passed to provide for the planning, development, and construction of housing for the needy, with some amendments to the laws specifically designed for older persons as, for example, the National Housing Act as amended. The major responsibility for carrying out these housing programs lies with the Department of Housing and Urban Development (HUD). This agency provides special funds for housing of older people.

Home Construction. Special funds for construction are provided in several ways. The first way is through direct long-term low interest loans to municipalities, such as cities or counties, to build apartment houses or other multidwelling complexes. These loans are designed to encourage municipalities to include old people in their public housing plans.

At first, in 1956, only municipalities were eligible to receive the loans, but since 1968 private nonprofit groups have also been eligible. This change has made it possible for religious and neighborhood organizations to become involved in the housing of older people and to attempt to meet the needs of the older residents in their buildings. Thus, the older residents received better housing and more social service and attention than before.

One important aspect of public housing for the elderly is that the monthly rents are limited to 25 percent of their income. In this way, if an older person has an income of $200 a month, his rent will be only $50. A person's rent usually includes utilities and heating costs. HUD's special funding for apartment house construction makes such low rentals possible.

Rent Subsidies. A more recent HUD development is a program known as Section 8. This program is not only for the elderly but for all whose income does not exceed certain amounts. Section 8 is also part of the amended National Housing Act.

Section 8 differs from earlier programs in that it pays for rent subsidies rather than for the construction of large apartment buildings. Landlords who participate in this program are paid the difference between the rent that a person can afford to pay and the rent a given apartment could fetch on the open market. Under some circumstances landlords are lent money to repair their buildings, if in turn they agree to participate in the Section 8 program for a specific period of time. One of the advantages to this program is that it enables older persons and others to choose the neighborhood and type of apartment he or she wants. Since Section 8 participants are scattered throughout different neighborhoods, they avoid the problems associated with high density public housing.

The different approaches to the funding of housing for the elderly have encouraged the development of many different types of programs, which is desirable because the housing needs of old and other persons are diverse, thus requiring many different types of solutions.

WHERE TO GO TO GET HELP

As indicated, the Older Americans Act includes services for recreation and leisure activities, congregate and home-delivered meals, information and referral, outreach, transportation, and legal assistance. These services are provided through a network of senior citizen centers. Except in isolated rural areas, these centers are usually accessible to a large number of people. The first, and also the easiest, place to check for assistance programs is in the local telephone directory under the listing for your city or county. If there are no programs listed, contact the local United Way/United Fund office. In many localities the United Way contributes money to senior citizen programs. If that office cannot supply the needed service, it can usually locate a service provider through an information and referral process.

Churches, unions, and fraternal organizations are also good places with which to check. They are frequently in touch with programs for older persons; sometimes they also provide direct assistance through meals-on-wheels programs, transportation services, and other help of this type.

For benefits through Title XX of the Social Security Act contact your nearest Social Security office. The address and telephone number can be found in your local telephone directory.

ACTION programs are generally organized in senior citizen centers, so this is the best place to contact if you are interested in RSVP, Foster Grandparents, or the Senior Companion Program. Since the Service Corps of Retired Executives is jointly administered, the Small Business Administration is a good place to check to see if there is a local program. ACTION also maintains a toll-free long distance number (800-424-8580) so that persons interested in participating in its programs can call for information.

Finally, if there are no local resources, it is worth calling or writing the State Office on Aging, usually located in the state's capital city. Since these offices are responsible for planning, administering, and funding local programs, they can generally put you in touch with the right provider. This is true also for Title XX and ACTION programs as well as for Older Americans Act services.

The situation for housing is somewhat different since a totally different federal agency is involved. In this case the best place to start is the local housing authority. Once again, check the telephone book for city or county housing authorities. If this strategy is unsuccessful, contact the regional federal HUD office and ask for assistance in locating local housing services. HUD can be found by looking in the telephone book for Housing and Urban Development, listed under United States Government.

In some rare instances, none of these strategies will work. In that case the following addresses may be useful:

U.S. Administration on Aging   ACTION
330 C Street S.W.   Washington, D.C. 20525
HEW South
Washington, D.C. 20201

REFERENCES

Barrow, G. and Smith, P. *Aging, Agism and Society.* West Publishing Co., St. Paul, Mn., 1979. Chapter 16.

Butler, R.N. and Lewis, M.I. *Aging and Mental Health.* The C.V. Mosby Co., St. Louis, Mo., 1977. Appendix C.

Hendricks, J. and Hendricks, C.C. *Aging in Mass Society.* Winthrop, Cambridge, 1977. Chapter 9.

Mayer, A.J. "The Graying of America." *Newsweek,* February 28, 1977.

Proceedings of the 1971 White House Conference on Aging. *Toward a National Policy on Aging.* U.S. Government Printing Office, 1973.

St. Louis Area Agency on Aging. *Guide to Social Services.* 1978.

Special Committee on Aging, United States Senate. *Developments in Aging.* June 1975.

Ward, R.A. *The Aging Experience.* J.B. Lippincott Co., New York, 1979. Chapter 12.

Chapter 5

Work, Retirement, and Leisure

The life pattern for most older men has been work, retirement, and leisure. For older women the pattern has been child-rearing and home maintenance, which is work; the empty nest situation, which is a type of semiretirement; and leisure, with a minimum of home maintenance. If life has been serene between husband and wife during the work phase, it may not be so during the retirement or empty nest phase and may become worse during the leisure phase. This is not to say that the post-work phases of life must have a negative effect on marital relations, it is just that sometimes this seems to be the case.

Since young women have now entered the work force in substantial numbers, and middle-aged women are now either entering or reentering it, marital relationships are taking different forms. Adjustments are required, especially when there is a transition from one phase to another. For example, the middle-aged woman may become interested in a new career just as her husband is tapering off from work and trying to spend more time with her. At the time that he is striving to develop more meaningful relations, she is focusing on self-fulfillment at work and a career. There can be adjustment problems, too, for the older, non-working wife whose husband has just retired, since there are now two of them facing a life of more leisure. The adjustment problems are seen in the humorous anecdote of the woman who now has the retired husband home much of the day, intruding upon her privacy and role of chief and sole organizer. "I married you for better or worse, but not for lunch everyday," she laments.

WORK

Since so much of life is spent at work, the quality of life and work satisfaction become almost synonymous. If the work is satisfying, people generally want to continue it as long as possible. If the work is not satisfying, people are glad to stop and retire. As might be expected, executives, managers, doctors, professors, and others with satisfying and prestigious positions tend to want to keep on working; factory workers, clerical workers, and unskilled laborers do not. Job satisfaction seems to center around whether or not the individual's abilities are maximally used.

To stop work can be hard. People, particularly men, are referred to not so much by who they are as by what they do for a living. Who are you? I am a doctor. What kind of a person is he? He is a laborer. For women, this is less true, but it also applies. Who are you? A teacher. What kind of a person is she? A housewife. Socioeconomic status and roles are implicit in these questions and answers. Often, so are feelings of self-worth and usefulness.

More and more women have been entering the work force and they are staying in it longer than men. Work seems to have a different meaning for women. More men are willing to retire than women; income is not as big a consideration for women in deciding whether or not they want to continue working. Many women choose to remain at work because it gives them a greater feeling of accomplishment than work at home. They get salaries which are not only income but tokens of reward for effort; they meet friends and socialize. They are individuals apart from their husbands and children. Not all women feel or want this, but it seems more and more do.

There are several problems older adults have with their desire to keep working. There is an assumption that the older worker is less healthy or less smart than the younger one. People often assume that the older worker is slipping on the job or just hanging on. All these suppositions may be false. Older workers very often carry out their job responsibilities as well as or better than younger workers; they tend to be more attached to their jobs. In general, work and work relationships mean role status and sociability. Loss of these can mean feeling down and isolated.

RETIREMENT

Societies mark the time when a child is thought to become an adult by either formal or informal ceremonies. It is a ritual or a rite. When a single person joins with another to form a family, this passage is marked by ceremony. The birth of babies is marked by rites of passage, as are deaths. Retirement may also be seen as a passage, but the ceremony, if any, is very individual and rarely, if ever, of a religious character as on the other occasions. Nevertheless, it is a crucial period of life.

There is another important difference between retirement and the other passages in life. The latter occur in just about all societies, but retirement occurs only in wealthy societies. Sickness may separate someone from the work force, but that is not quite the same thing as retirement. In poorer countries, and years ago also in the U.S., retirement was only for a small handful of wealthy people. Now, in the United States, it is for the vast majority. Union and business pension plans, Social Security, and other government supports make this possible. At present, retirement is mandatory at age 70 for all but relatively few people in special occupations, or for the self-employed; it used to be at age 65. It is likely that we will do away with mandatory age retirement in the future; some 14 states have already done so, but at present, mandatory age retirement is the law in most areas.

Individual Considerations

Voluntary and Involuntary Retirement. Some people want to retire and some do not. When people retire involuntarily, there tends to be anguish and even fear. Satisfactory retirement is possible when there is sufficient income, when health is good, and when there is enough to do to fill the time well. Health is important in more ways than is at first apparent. Just as successful adjustment to a new job calls for vigor and energetic application, so does the successful adjustment to retirement, a different type of assignment, a type that is rarely experienced before in the adult lifetime. Some people who are forced to retire never give themselves a chance to do well in retirement. The workaholic, the person who never develops outside interests, whose personal identity is completely wrapped up in the job, and who resists retirement to the point of avoiding preretirement planning, is a poor candidate for successful retirement.

However, there is a whole world of people who cannot wait to retire. Persons in heavy labor, or with boring assembly line jobs, those whose talents are either not used or whose skills are limited, those whose income from work is not much different from what their retirement income would be, look forward to retirement—and it is clearly voluntary.

Voluntary or not, retirement without planning for it, without preparation, bodes ill for success. Financial planning is vital; activities to be pursued in retirement must be given attention, new ones may even have to be learned; social relations on the job must take on a new character. All this requires forethought, otherwise retirement becomes a life of boredom, restlessness, and even depression. Fortunately, there are now preparation-for-retirement seminars and counseling opportunities in many larger business institutions. Private groups also have been established for this purpose. Unfortunately, such opportunities for preparation are not yet available to the majority of wage earners.

Phases of Retirement. Butler and Lewis indicate that several phases to retirement exist. First, there is anticipation. This could be positive or not, depending on whether retirement is voluntary or not. But even if it is voluntary, changes are taking place on the job that are often negative. Other employees, for instance, start pulling away socially in preparation for the parting; they begin to plan for a successor. The soon-to-be-retired person's job may also be a source of infighting among coworkers and friends. The atmosphere at work is no longer quite the same.

The second phase of retirement is the actual day that has either been dreaded or looked forward to with pleasure, the day of separation. This can be an emotional event but it is short-lived. The next phase is the most difficult one, the period where adjustments have to be made as a new life is being established. Things are different and, like it or not, changes have to be made. These changes can vary from a new career, hobbies, and interests, long neglected because of lack of time, to idleness with boredom and nothing to do. Idleness may be fine for some, but not for many.

The fourth and last phase is the acceptance of a new life. For better or worse, there is finally recognition that another life passage has been completed.

Societal Considerations

Most men and women in their sixties, seventies, and beyond seem to have the physical and mental capacity to continue on their jobs. Mandatory or compulsory retirement, therefore, takes the form of violation of civil rights. To many, mandatory retirement is wrong; it must be discontinued. This argument has made for some strange bedfellows. A 1977 article by Jerry Flint of the *New York Times News Service* reported that both the right-wing actor John Wayne and the American Civil Liberties Union lined up against compulsory age retirement. The coalition on the other side was equally unlikely—it included both the AFL-CIO, and the Chamber of Commerce of the United States. Both favored compulsory age retirement. The battle is not over, but it seems that those against compulsory age retirement are winning. Government workers' mandatory retirement at age 70 was eliminated, and the 65-year-old limit of work in most places of employment was moved up to 70. As indicated, 14 states removed age as a basis of forced retirement. Discrimination based on age is against the law.

Who are the good guys and who are the bad in the argument for or against mandatory age retirement? There are good arguments on both sides. One set of arguments deals with humanistic considerations, the other mainly with economic ones. On the side of humanism, it is obvious that to cut someone off from the work force when he is still competent and wants to work—and may be miserable not working—is just plain unkind. It is unkind and, depending on the economic picture, may also be unnecessary.

On the side of economics, the arguments are changing. The economic picture changes and with it attitudes toward mandatory age retirement change. During the depression of the 1930s, the goal was to woo older people away from their jobs to make their jobs available to younger people. Social Security benefits were established to ease the exit of the older workers. Opening up jobs for younger people is still one of the reasons given in favor of mandatory retirement. During World War II, when there were many jobs and few workers, older people were encouraged to stay at work as long as the situation permitted and were even given opportunity to do volunteer work, to contribute to the war effort.

The current emphasis on doing away with mandatory age

retirement seems to be based on a combination of humanistic values and economic predictions based on demographic trends, that is, changes in statistical characteristics of populations. In the course of the next 20 years or so, it is expected that the number of people past 65 years of age will rise appreciably, while the number of workers younger than 40 is expected to decline. Therefore, we will need the older workers; also, there may not be as many young workers to push the older ones out. In addition, the argument goes, not many older adults with an opportunity to retire will want to stay on in view of their improved pensions. Most important, the Social Security system is such that those still in the work force pay to support the retired worker. As more and more people retire, and as fewer young people join the work force and contribute to the Social Security system, retirement funds may run out. Keeping the older worker at work reduces the drain on the Social Security retirement fund.

The other side of this story is that many unions and large business concerns fear that older workers will not choose to retire, and younger workers therefore will not get a chance for promotion. Furthermore, they fear that minorities and women may not get an opportunity for jobs they were unable to get before because of discrimination. "Dead wood," those who never contributed much to their jobs, cannot be easily pushed out without compulsory retirement. However, this fear on the part of unions and management may not be based on fact, at least as it applies to the average worker. With pensions and other financial opportunities, there is an increasing trend toward retiring at a younger age, rather than an older one. This trend, however, may reverse with severe inflation because most pensioners are on fixed incomes.

Unions and large businesses also fear that the elderly workers who had once been effective, but lost that effectiveness because of ill health or other changes due to age, could be weeded out only with great difficulty, if at all. This is not to say that all older workers can be expected to fall down on the job. Just the opposite, many corporations have found the mix of old and young workers just right because of the experience of the old and advanced education and skills of the young. Nevertheless, there are some elderly who do decline on the job. At some point in life, everyone experiences some decline even if it sets in only at a very advanced age. Further, it would seem that managements of large corporations, businesses, and institutions would do well to refresh their upper echelon positions with new blood.

Contrary to popular opinion, it is very difficult to assess the job performance of older workers and make such assessment rather than age the basis of retirement. It might be more desirable to train persons for leisure time pursuits and readjustment of values with respect to work and leisure, and to stop trying to keep them in the workforce until very late in life.

LEISURE

Once the child becomes an adult, leisure time activity is something sandwiched between long periods of work and responsibility. This is not true for each and every person, but even the idle rich, by and large, are not without major time consuming work responsibilities. The retired person, similar to the child, has the opportunity for lengthy leisure time activity, into which work responsibility, if desired, can be fitted. Leisure time can be a fun period and it can be a bore.

Leisure time activity is not synonymous with having nothing to do. The retired old person with nothing to do, like the teenager with nothing to do, becomes irritable, moody, complaining. Both can get into trouble. The active older person, like the active teenager, can be interesting, even exciting. The trick about leisure time is to fill it with activity that is enjoyable, meaningful, and healthy. "Mickey Mouse" tasks—activities done just for the sake of doing something—do not work. If arts and crafts, for example, are not your thing, then such activities are just as well left alone. If you like to paint and make things, then arts and crafts are just fine. Leisure time activity must be personally rewarding. Leisure time can be as hard and as demanding as a job, or it can be relaxing, but above all, it must be enjoyable, and even more importantly, personally meaningful.

Among the leisure time activities people of all ages should engage in is physical exercise. Physical health, mobility (even including the simple ability to walk), and feelings of well-being derive from exercise. Continuous and even strenuous daily exercises lasting 20 to 30 minutes is recommended for all, provided they have a doctor's approval. The vigor of the exercise should vary with physical status as, for example, walking versus bicycling versus jogging. Less vigorous exercise over longer periods, such as gardening, should supplement this. Reading, attending classes and lectures, engaging in hobbies and watching television are all to the good, if they are mixed with physical exercise.

Work and leisure are not always easy to tell apart. Leisure time and work time activities are generally distinguished by what is considered enjoyable and voluntary and what is seen as necessary and mandatory. However, the distinction between obligation and enjoyable voluntary activity is not totally adequate in distinguishing between work and leisure. One and the same activity is work for one person and play for another. Kalish, for example, points out that he dislikes gardening; for him it is work. Others enjoy gardening. Jogging or other strenuous activity may be a necessary and voluntary leisure time pursuit for many, but not exactly an enjoyable one. Still, it cannot be classed as work. One thing is clear about the leisure time activity of old people: it is hard to tell how satisfactory it is by just appearance. The old man sitting on a park bench talking with friends may be bored, but he may also be doing exactly what he wants, even though he has an opportunity to do something else. The older adult who is doing volunteer work may seem to be doing exactly what he wants and enjoying it, but, on the other hand, he may hate it, and not know what else to do; yet, this is preferable to doing nothing with so much time on hand.

What constitutes good leisure time activity is very individual. The important thing is to fill time enjoyably and, it is hoped, constructively. There are several ways of categorizing free time activity; Ward lists 12 characteristics which relate to how satisfactory the activity is for the individual. Free time activity varies in whether or not it involves (1) self-direction, (2) creativity, (3) enjoyment, (4) opportunities to develop talent, (5) productive outlets, (6) physical energy, (7) similarities to work, (8) other people, (9) service to others, (10) prestige, (11) tension, and perhaps most important, (12) whether or not the activity fits into the lifestyle of the retired person.

Leisure, like the economic aspects of retirement, must involve planning. Some people in their retirement are blessed with a wide variety of interests, but others are cursed with too much time. For the retired worker, time is an available commodity.

REFERENCES

Aiken, L. *Later Life.* W.B. Saunders Co., Philadelphia, 1978. Chapter 7.

Butler, R.N. and Lewis, M.I. *Aging and Mental Health.* The C.V. Mosby Co., St. Louis, Mo., 1977. Chapter 6.

Kalish, R.A. *Late Adulthood: Perspectives on Human Development.* Brooks/Cole, Monterey, Calif., 1975. Chapter 5.

Rogers, D. *The Adult Years.* Prentice Hall, Inc. Englewood Cliffs, N.J., 1979. Chapter 10.

Sheppard, H.L. "Work and Retirement." *Handbook of Aging and the Social Sciences,* edited by R.H. Binstock and E. Shanas. Van Nostrand Reinhold Co., New York, 1976.

Ward, R.A. *The Aging Experience.* J.B. Lippincott Co., New York, 1979. Chapter 7.

Chapter 6

Money

In many instances when people stop working and retire, their income is very much reduced. More than that, the working man can rarely save enough to sustain him in old age. Additional money therefore must come from some other source. In the old days, adult sons and daughters were expected to take care of the old mother and father; in fact, young parents wanted many children, at least in part, to help support them in their old age. Now, the vast majority of Americans feel that children should not be expected to support their old parents.

SAVINGS AND PENSIONS

How do old people support themselves when they no longer receive regular paychecks? First, many people have savings and investment income. Unfortunately, many more could have saved for old age than did, but were not prudent enough to do so. Second, work and union sources provide pensions, some providing a substantial income. However, when it comes right down to it, only a minority of workers are covered by pensions. Third, there is support from the government. This support is assuming more and more importance, because more and more needs are being covered.

SOCIAL SECURITY

In 1935, under President Roosevelt, a major innovation was begun. A new federal government program was instituted which made it possible, for the first time in the United States, for a large number of old people to have some minimal retirement income. The Social Security system was begun in a modest way and has expanded considerably since then (see Chapter 4).

Retirement Checks

The Social Security system is unique. Retirement payments to older adults are not supported by the general pool of income taxes as are the other public needs and services. Instead, money is taken from the paychecks of all workers and combined with money from the employer to form the basis of the monthly Social Security checks which older people receive in retirement. This system may sound unfair to the young, but actually it is not, because young workers can look forward to getting their Social Security checks from the contribution of the new generations of young workers when they are elderly. This program of the young generation helping the older one has worked well in the past, but a new demographic situation may make trouble in the future, unless careful watching and intelligent planning takes place.

The potential problem lies in the fact that more and more people are reaching the age where they could retire and get Social Security benefits. As the number of retirees increases, especially in proportion to the number of young workers in the workforce, fewer people are earning salaries from which Social Security money is drawn to pay the increasing number of older people. The system works well as long as there is enough money from younger workers coming in to pay for the older persons' retirement years. It can break down if not enough money comes in. It may be necessary to change the character of the Social Security program sometime in the future, but it is inconceivable that economic help for the elderly in one form or another could be discontinued. In fact, what is much more likely is that more and varied economic help will be forthcoming.

Social Security benefits are not charity, nor are they welfare payments; they are the result of payments the recipient made through deductions on his earnings while he worked. This point might have been more important in 1935 when the program was established than it is today when we have a more tolerant view of government help than we did at that time.

Who Gets the Checks? Old people are not the only ones to benefit from the Social Security system. Young people can receive checks too (see below). Both young and old, however, have to meet certain requirements to receive the money.

Today, more than nine out of every ten working people in the United States are building protection for themselves and their families under the Social Security system. Social Security benefits have been extended to most self-employed people, most state and local employees, members of the Armed Forces, and others, but not federal civil service workers. Who is eligible for Social Security retirement checks? Those who pass the Retirement Test, which is based on age, earnings, and history of past employment.

Age. Everyone who has the minimum required work history and is over the age of 62 is eligible for retirement checks, *if* he or she has retired. Retirement here means anyone who is not gainfully employed, earning more than a certain amount at work. Money received outside of work income is not considered work earnings. In 1979, to receive retirement checks when younger than 65, earned income could not be greater than $3,480 a year. From age 65 to age 72, the most that could be earned while remaining eligible for Social Security retirement benefits was $4,500. After age 72, there is eligibility with full-time employment and no limit in earnings. By 1982, full employment and eligibility will be allowed at age 70.

The older worker under 72 can continue to work full time, of course, and receive full salary; he will receive no Social Security retirement checks, however, if the salary is above the limit. In fact, Social Security payments will be deducted from the paycheck.

How Much Are the Monthly Checks? During 1979 the monthly checks ranged from $133 to almost $500, depending on the person's work history and age. The exact amount changes because the yearly benefits are now based on the cost of living. As inflation increases so do the checks. The exact amount also depends on the retirement age; it increases the later a person chooses to start receiving the benefits. At age 62, the benefits are only 80 percent of the benefits at age 65. The reduced amount, that is, 80 percent, is permanent; it does not go up at age 65. There is a three percent increase in dollar payments for each year after age 62 that retirement is declared. In other words, if Social Security retirement checks are claimed at age 63, the amount will be three percent higher than at 62; if they are claimed at age 64, they will be six percent higher than at age 62, and so on.

The exact amount of the monthly checks also depends on the work history. A person must have credit for a certain amount of work time. Anyone who became 62 in 1979 needed to have received work credits ranging from seven to ten years. Within limits, the higher the earnings, the greater the retirement benefits.

Survivors' Checks

The Social Security system today hardly resembles the system at its start. But even during the very early days, it was recognized that when the retired worker died, all the checks that had been received would not take care of the family's needs. In 1939, the Social Security survivor benefit plan was added. It is a type of insurance plan. Young children of the worker can receive payments and, in some cases, so can the surviving husband or wife. It is possible for the surviving wife to receive 100 percent of the deceased husband's benefits. A divorced spouse, grandchildren, or parents of the deceased worker can also qualify for the checks. The amount of survivor payments depends on the earned income of the survivor.

A widow or widower can get survivor checks as early as age 60. A divorced wife can also receive payments at this age but the marriage has to have lasted at least ten years. If the surviving spouse is under age 60 and takes care of a deceased worker's child who is under 18 and receiving Social Security payments, she, too, can qualify for benefits.

Disability Insurance

In 1956, almost 20 years after the Social Security program was begun, disability insurance was initiated. This is not an older person's insurance, but it is for everyone. Part of the Social Security contribution from paychecks goes for disability insurance. To get disability benefits, a worker 31 or older must be fully insured and have a certain amount of work credit. If disability occurs before age 31, proportionately less work credit is required.

Medicare

It was not until 1965 that Medicare, a health insurance program was instituted. There are two parts to the program: hospital insurance and medical insurance. People over 65 are eligible for this coverage, as are young people who are disabled if they had been receiving disability payments for two or more years.

The hospital insurance pays for inpatient hospital care and some kinds of follow-up care. The medical insurance helps pay the costs of doctors' services, outpatient hospital services, and certain other medical items. These coverages help a lot but they do not come close to taking care of much of the medical help older people need. This is the reason why a comprehensive national health insurance plan seems inevitable.

PROGRAMS BASED ON NEED

Social Security, as we pointed out before, is not welfare. Social Security payments are based on worker contributions, with the amounts specified by law. Supplemental security income (SSI) assures a minimum monthly income to needy people over 65, or those who are blind or disabled. Eligibility is based solely on income and assets. Such payments are made from general tax revenues, not from worker paycheck contributions, but the Social Security Administration disburses funds.

Another source of aid for the elderly is Medicaid, not to be confused with Medicare. Medicare is health insurance based on worker contribution. Medicaid, like SSI, is based on economic need.

THE PUBLIC-PRIVATE MIX

It is evident that between private pensions, savings, and investments on one hand, and Social Security and other public programs on the other, the majority of the elderly is not without funds, although it is not always so. It is only fair that a humanitarian society provides for its members in old age. The Social Security Administration is a helpful body. Information is available and personal interviews may be arranged by phoning the local Social Security office.

Economic problems remain, nevertheless. Not all old people know how to get the help they have earned and need so badly. Inflation has eaten into fixed incomes. The Medicare program, as helpful as it is, covers only a small portion of total medical costs. In the end, many of the old remain poor and needy. We have a long way to go in making things right for the old but we have come a long way already.

REFERENCES

Schulz, J.H. "Income Distribution and the Aging." *Handbook of Aging and the Social Sciences,* edited by R.H. Binstock and E. Shanas. Van Nostrand Reinhold Co., New York, 1976.

Ward, R.A. *The Aging Experience.* J.B. Lippincott Co., New York, 1979. Chapter 6.

U.S. Department of Health, Education and Welfare. Publication Nos. (SSA): 78-10033, April, 1978; 78-10072, June, 1978; 78-10084, June, 1978; 78-10035, Aug., 1978; 79-10048, Jan., 1979.

Chapter 7

Contentment in Old Age

Much attention has been directed to the study of contentment in old age. The aim of such studies was to learn what adjustments and changes could be made before becoming old which could make life better later on. The study goals have gone by several names, such as life satisfaction, morale, successful aging, and happiness. These studies report interesting and important things, but the prescription for contentment remains unknown, except in very general terms. In the end, the prescription must be in individual terms for it to be helpful.

THE BASIC INGREDIENTS

It seems that three ingredients are needed for contentment in old age; they are obvious and have already been mentioned. Two of them are sufficient income and reasonably good health, which have already been discussed in detail.

The third ingredient necessary for contentment is to have someone to talk to and confide in. This has also been discussed, but only indirectly in terms of the importance of family and friends. People, today as in the past, tend to stay with family. The *multigenerational family*, that is, the household with two or more generations living together, is as prevalent today as it was in the past, contrary to popular opinion. The multigenerational family seems to come about when there is a death in the nuclear family, or when money is very short. As indicated in Chapter 3, older people tend to prefer not to live in this way but they do want to live close to their family members. They want friends and they tend to find them among the old rather than the young. Young people, including younger family members, often make for tensions and clashes. Loud stereos, new values, and styles regarding work, clothes, and politics are often sources of conflict.

People of every age need someone to be close to. The husband or wife is usually that close confidant. When either dies, the confidant is lost. Widowed people are living alone more and more often, not with children or other relatives. Unscrupulous people often take advantage of them. This is more true of aged widows than young ones. They are alone and often without anyone to talk with or be close to.

Big adjustments need to be made as a result of the grief of being left without a spouse. The adjustments are different for men and women. The man alone must now do things that he never did before or, perhaps, that he felt he should not do. He now has to take care of the home, do the shopping, laundry, and the cooking. The woman alone must now take care of business matters and meet the world without an escort. This is very difficult for many old women, some of whom never even learned to write a check. Such adjustments, fortunately, may not be nearly as much a problem for future generations of widowed elderly as they are for many current elderly widows and widowers.

For old people who are now or who will be living alone, confidants are needed for contentment. Without them, severe depression sometimes sets in. No matter how busy a person is, no matter how many clubs are visited or hobbies undertaken, the need for a confidant remains. In fact, with a confidant, the number of clubs and hobbies attended, or activities engaged in can be reduced to very little with life satisfaction still possible.

Having these three ingredients—health, money, and some-one to confide in—does not guarantee contentment. They are necessary but other things are also needed.

ARE OLD PEOPLE DISCONTENT?

Perhaps this chapter should have started out with the question of whether or not old people are discontent and dissatisfied. Only a few studies have asked this question, but their results seem to agree by saying, "Life is not all that bad." For example, one study found that older people saw their own lives as better than the average person's. In another study, a full 20 percent of the elderly felt that the best years were "now." A third study found greater satisfaction and happiness among both young and older adults than among middle-aged adults. In other words, old age need not be a bad time in life: it can be a good time. One investigator reviewed the literature and concluded that satisfaction with life may be a personality characteristic not necessarily associated with age.

WHAT IS CONTENTMENT IN OLD AGE?

What is contentment or happiness? Kalish has discussed this question in the context of successful aging by listing four definitions that are often assumed to be correct, although this is not necessarily the case.

The "Right" Way of Life

The successful older person, the person most likely to be content, is the person who follows the rules of behavior that society says is right. What the older person feels like doing, what he believes, is not the issue. Of concern is what has come to be known as *age norms* and *age constraints*—expectations of what older people ought not to do and cannot do. These expectations really govern the lives of many older people. Age norms and age constraints set older people in a mold, keeping them from doing what younger people can and are even encouraged to do. A group of investigators, Neugarten, Moore, and Lowe, gave examples of this: "He's too old to be working so hard;" or "She's too young to wear that style of clothing." The phrase "Act your age" is often heard when an old person feels like being a little bit silly. Think about it: Should a 70-year-old woman on a beach wear a bikini? Why not? Should she be seen dancing at a disco in tight slacks, if she feels like it? Why not? Age norms and age constraints do not make for happiness. They keep a person from being himself or herself; they keep people from being active and outgoing.

Act Middle-Aged: Keep Busy

The old person is successful and happy if he or she acts similar to the way he or she did when younger. Think young, act middle-aged when old, and you will be happier, this definition of successful aging suggests. The fact is, the older person may not feel like being middle-aged, busy, and responsible to many. He may want to pull away and should be allowed to. He may be more content not doing what he did years ago.

Disengagement Theory. One of the most active areas of research in gerontology was based on a theory called *disengagement*. This theory was developed on the basis of important research but later came under attack.

Research showed that many old people, maybe even most old people, become withdrawn, that they pull away or disengage from other people and from activity. They keep to themselves. Seeing this, the researchers said that this is normal for them. To keep older people happy, they said, let them follow inner-directed interests and feelings. Let them disengage, even encourage them to do so. Do not make an effort to bring older people out.

Later research suggested that many old people withdraw not because they like to be this way, but because they have no choice. The world keeps them out. It is mainly the sick and those without means that are disengaged. Disengagement, therefore, is not the normal process; it is a process that is forced on the older person.

Activity Theory. The next recommendation, therefore, was to get the older person out of his disengaged state. Keep him active. Activity will make for good morale; it is the only way to contentment, some people insisted.

Different Kinds of People. Later research pointed to what might have been obvious in the first place. There are all kinds of people; some like to disengage and some not. Help them do what is best for them. It makes more sense to find out how a person feels about himself than to tell him how to behave and what to do. This is not always simple to do. Asking questions does not always disclose the whole story. How does a person judge his happiness? Expectations play a role, as do his past feelings. One person may have a whole lot more to be happy about than the next but just does not feel as satisfied.

Self-respect, or self-esteem, is important here. Low self-esteem can cause depression. Some elderly people have taken on the negative stereotypes about old people which are held by young people with whom they live. Many of the elderly had had these negative attitudes themselves when they were young and cannot shake them off now that they are old and should know better. Believing that they are unworthy, many elderly cut themselves off from rewarding situations and feel unvalued. This can be a self-fulfilling pattern of discontent.

Feeling Satisfied About the Present

The third definition or conception of the contented older person rests with the idea that if he has all the ingredients—health, money, and a confidant—and is as active as he was at middle age, he will be happy. Life is not all that simple. There are many people of all ages who have the ingredients and are still discontent.

Feeling Satisfied About the Present and Past

It is most unlikely that the older person can achieve peace and contentment if he or she is displeased with how life has been spent. It is also unlikely that contentment can be achieved if present behavior is regarded as bad. Old people, it seems, spend a lot of time in reminiscence. There is a life review to try to resolve old matters that still bother and hurt. This is somewhat different from the middle-aged person who reminisces merely for the purpose of solving current problems.

Reminiscence does not always result in self-acceptance. People think about the past, try to relate it to the present and future, and see limitations as well as successes. Obviously, the more pleasant the reminiscence, the fewer the limitations, and the greater the successes, the more likely is contentment in old age.

Life review is similar except that here the person is not idly recalling the past, but has a purpose. There is effort to bring up unresolved things of the past that bother and hurt. Impending death hastens the life review because little time is left to arrange and resolve things. A life review can make for depression and anxiety in people who have been mean to others and hurt them in the past. Failing to come to grips with these behaviors in the process of the life review results in a discontented old person. Resolution and acceptance of problems and conflicts of the past make contentment possible.

FEARS REGARDING OLD AGE

People, young and old, have fears about aging and old age. Fears can make what would otherwise be a life of contentment into a life of anxiety and discomfort. This is a pity because while some fears are realistic, others are not. In either case, fears serve little constructive purpose.

Old and young share some of the same fears about old age, mostly concerning sickness and impairment. The young also have other concerns, most of which are totally unnecessary.

Fears of the Young

Appearance. Young people, certainly middle-aged people, are often afraid of losing their looks. Hair whitens, skin wrinkles, stomachs bulge, postures stoop. This all happens—so what? Why should we judge good looks on the basis of youth? We live in a society that values youth and youthful appearances. TV, newspaper, and magazine advertisements strengthen this conception. Appearances of the old should be judged by criteria suitable for them. What is so special and desirable about the very thin, long-legged model? What is so detrimental about the elderly looking different from the young? The value of people does not rest in properties that are only skin deep. What is better about one skin than another?

Sexuality. Young people are afraid of losing their looks, and many seem to be afraid of losing their sexuality. This fear has been termed a myth, because sexuality is rarely lost. The study of sexuality in old age has received a lot of attention, probably because it is of so much concern to many.

The idea of sexual relations among the elderly is an uncomfortable one for many young people. As Butler and Lewis point out, we like to think of grandmother in the kitchen baking cookies and of grandfather in his rocking chair smoking a pipe. We do not like to think of our grandparents in terms of sexual relations. It seems we do not even like to have scientists learning about our elders if it involves asking them questions having to do with sex. As seen in at least one study, middle-aged family members withdrew their aged parents from the investigation when such questioning began, despite the fact that the parents volunteered. Man and wife are often separated in state hospitals or homes for the aged, another sign of discomfort regarding sexuality in later life.

Older people are interested in sex and it is as much a part of their nature as it is of younger people. What changes is how sexually active most older people want to be, which is no different from other psychobiological activities. For example, the older person's interests are likely to wane when it comes to partaking in active sports; sex is just another psycho-biological interest.

There is no evidence that women's sexuality diminishes until age 60, and then, if at all, the decline is very small. Men decline more, at least in terms of frequency of sexual activity, but it is gradual, starting in the teens. However, even at age 80 and above, there is still an ability to enjoy sexual relations. Perhaps more than psychobiological diminition of interest and frequency, what limits sexual gratification of many older people is the absence of a partner. Most sexual activity occurs between man and wife, and many wives outlive their mates by many years.

Fear of the Old

Back in 1968, the magazine of Johns Hopkins University reported an interesting study where 600 elderly alumni were asked how they felt about aging and what their reactions were to it. On the whole, the alumni tended to be positive about this stage of their lives, but they reported some changes, mainly physical. They were most afraid of their physical conditions getting worse. One person said that there was much pleasure in growing old, "if the body holds up; however, the body lets one down badly." Others feared that they would become a burden to friends and family because of ill health.

Sex did not seem to be an issue; fear of death was not very prominent, perhaps surprisingly, but fear of living with great physical deterioration was. This fear included loss of independence. Family, friends, and lack of pressures were among the pleasures noted, time and time again. One woman said even the physical problems would not be so bad if people stopped mentioning her aged physical status.

At least as noted among these exceptional alumni, the aged can be said to have much contentment, but there is a constant fear that this state may stop.

SUMMING UP

Any one definition of successful aging or a prescription for being content in old age is bound to be inadequate. It is an individual thing. Yet, certain factors are important and this chapter has tried to bring them together. There are three basic ingredients necessary to contentment in old age—reasonable health, adequate income, and someone to be close to and talk to. There are family members and friends, but there must also be a confidant.

Some elderly people like to disengage and others do not. Often, old people are disengaged against their will; society pushes them out. People cannot be content in old age if they wish to be active but are not permitted to, or conversely, if they want to disengage, but are not allowed to.

Contentment in old age is possible only when unrealistic and unnecessary fears are controlled. Fears of looking different than one did when young are just plain foolish fears; fears of losing the ability to have and enjoy sexual relations are unfounded; fears concerning severe physical and mental impairment may someday come true for any person, but 80 percent of old people will not suffer in this way.

Fears must be kept under rational control. This is not easy to do. Past conflicts and unresolved problems must also be dealt with; the life review is useful in this regard. Conflict resolution and self-acceptance are keys to contentment. Contentment in old age is not only possible, it is even to be expected.

REFERENCES

Anonymous. "What's It Like?" *The Johns Hopkins Magazine.* Spring, 1968, 27-28.

Berardo, F.M. "Survivorship and Social Isolation: The Case of the Aged Widower." *Family Coordinator.* 1970, 19, 11-25.

Borges, M.A. and Dutton, L.J. "Attitudes Toward Aging." *The Gerontologist.* 1976, 16, 220-224.

Botwinick, J. *Aging and Behavior.* Springer Publishing Co., New York, 1978. Chapters 4 and 5.

Butler, R.N. and Lewis, M.I. *Aging and Mental Health.* The C.V. Mosby Co., St. Louis, Mo., 1977. Chapter 3.

Butler, R.N. and Lewis, M.I. *Love and Sex After Sixty.* Harper and Row, Publishers, New York, 1977.

Chown, S.M. "Morale, Careers and Personal Potentials." *Handbook of the Psychology of Aging.* edited by J.E. Birren and K.W. Schaie. Van Nostrand Reinhold Co., New York, 1977.

Cumming, E. and Henry, W. *Growing Old: The Process of Disengagement.* Basic Books, New York, 1961.

Kalish, R.A. *Late Adulthood: Perspectives on Human Development.* Brooks/Cole Publishing Co., Monterey, Ca., 1975. Chapter 3.

Lieberman, L.R. "Life Satisfaction in the Young and Old." *Psychological Reports.* 1970, 27, 75-79.

Lowenthal, M.F. and Haven, C. "Interaction and Adaptation Intimacy as a Critical Variable." *American Sociological Review.* 1968, 33, 20-30.

Masters, W.H. and Johnson, V.E. *Human Sexual Response.* Little, Brown and Co., Boston, 1966.

Neugarten, B.L. Moore, J.W., and Lowe, J.C. "Age Norms, Age Constraints and Adult Socialization." *Middle Age and Aging.* edited by B.L. Neugarten. University of Chicago Press, Chicago, 1968.

Pearson, J.S. "Age and Sex Differences Related to MMPI Response Frequency in 25,000 Medical Patients." *American Journal of Psychiatry.* 1965, 121, 988-995.

Pfeiffer, E. "Sexual Behavior in Old Age." *Behavior and Adaptation in Late Life.* edited by E. Pfeiffer and E.W. Busse. Little, Brown and Co., Boston, 1969.

Chapter 8

Development Across the Ages

There are two opposing views of how development unfolds across the life span. One view is that there are life stages, i.e., steps that must be climbed one by one. Once one stage is reached there is no return to the previous one, nor is there a need for it. Each stage represents an accomplishment where the task of the previous stage has been completed or the problem solved. The other view is that life is not so predictable. There are too many irregularities.

STAGE THEORIES

The Consistent Patterns of Life

The different stages of life are thought to have a type of biological force underlying them. There is a universality, a uni-directional pattern with no zigzagging. Stage theorists believe that everyone goes through these same stages and that this holds true for all societies and across all generations. A true stage theory is so exacting that the sociologist Kohlberg, who introduced the stage theory of moral development, maintained that even one exception to stage patterning questions the validity of the whole theory.

Stage theories have long been with us, but until fairly recently they have related only to children's growing up, for example, Freud's theory of psychosexual development or Piaget's theory of cognitive development. Most of these stage theories have suggested that development was completed around the teens. With the growing interest in middle age and old age, new stage theories have come into being.

There is a type of study which in some ways is similar to the stage theory study but is not identical to it. While stage theories assume a universal, unidirectional unfolding of life, there is a type of study which investigates adjustment to life events as they occur in particular societies. For example, there is an adjustment to the transition to marriage, to the empty nest period, to retirement, widowhood, and so on. Such studies are sometimes referred to as stage theory studies, but this is really not what they are because these transitions are not universal or unidirectional. Not all people, nor all societies, for that matter, experience empty nest or retirement syndromes. The results of such studies, more properly called adjustment studies rather than stage theory studies, have already been discussed, particularly in Chapters 2 and 7. In this chapter, we will focus on stage theories and the different personality characteristics they suggest.

Irregularity and Diversity of Life

Before considering stage theories, it is well to note that although it seems that most scientists accept the reasonableness of a stage theory, at least one prominent investigator does not. The results of Neugarten's studies and those of her colleagues point in other directions. Neugarten does not see age related regularities of life as the stage theory demands but instead sees increasing irregularities and a diversity of life patterns.

Neugarten sees the rhythms of life changing. People are

entering the labor force later because more people are pursuing extended educations. Women are entering the labor force but often go to school afterward. Men become fathers and grandfathers during the same year. The course of adult human development is too varied and irregular to tie it down to stages. There can be no "How to" or "Dr. Spock" book for adults, she insists.

The counter argument is that these varied life events do not change the picture of stage development. The tasks of each stage remain the same, only people cope with these tasks in different ways and at different times of life. Stage theorists would insist that successful entry to the next stage—whether as a father or grandfather—can come about only after the problems of the previous stage have been successfully handled. What Neugarten is referring to, stage theorists might insist, is adjustment studies, and these clearly point to irregularities.

Ego Development

Some stage theories start out with issues of development in infancy, then proceed to young childhood, childhood, adolescence, and stop there. Others continue to young adulthood and do not go beyond the twenties. There are now at least four stage theories that go to middle age, and one that goes to old age. Each of these sees each stage as a job to be completed or a crisis to overcome.

Erikson's stage theory of ego development is the oldest of the four theories that extends into middle age. It includes old age as a stage and is the one most frequently referred to in the literature on aging. The psychiatrist Erikson describes eight stages of man, each based on a need or crisis that must be met. If the decisions during one stage are valid, a successful adaptation can be made in the next. The first five stages cover infancy to adolescence. If the crises of development are successfully met, the unfolding person acquires first, in early infancy, a sense of trust. Then, in later infancy, autonomy is achieved. In early childhood initiative develops. A sense of industry and competence is characteristic of middle childhood, and, finally, personal identity is achieved in adolescence.

The sixth stage deals with young adulthood; the seventh with middle age; and the eighth with old age. The need in young adulthood is to give of oneself and to take from someone else as, for instance, in marriage. Children and work are major ingredients of this stage. Middle age focuses on guiding the next generation and encompasses a stage called generativity. There is dependence on the young because without having the opportunity or ability to give to the young, there is over self-indulgence or self-concern, a babying of oneself. This makes for an immature adult.

The final stage, ego-integrity, focuses on self-acceptance. Failure to do this leads to despair, a condition not all people can avoid. Coping with this stage or crisis is possible only when important matters have been settled and the successes and failures of life been accepted. The life review (see Chapter 7) makes such acceptance possible. Erickson suggests that good adjustment at this late point in life involves a type of fatalism, an acceptance of order in life, where even death is viewed without agony.

Life Structures and Time Zones

A newer stage theory is based on the concept of life structure. Life structure is seen as a basic pattern of a person's life at a given period of time. It is the relationship between the self and the world. The psychologist Levinson proposed this stage theory and focused on what has since become a popular concept in newspapers, magazines, and living room discussions, the idea of mid-life crisis.

Levinson sees the job of a person during the period from the late teens to the young twenties as separation from family in order to form a basis for living in the world. During his twenties a person gains entrance into the adult world where it is important to test what has been accomplished. Moving on to the mid-thirties, life becomes more stable and satisfying. There is a settling down. From the late thirties to the mid-forties, however, there has to be a review and reappraisal because of entrance into mid-life. There is not much time for reappraisal because crucial choices must be made. Levinson's studies have suggested to him that at this point in life, as many as 80 percent of men undergo a "tumultuous struggle" within themselves—the mid-life crisis. Levinson studied only 40 men; so, it is fair to ask: is the mid-life crisis really so much of an expected phenomenon as to constitute a true stage in human development?

A stage theory by Gould is remarkably similar in many ways. The details vary somewhat, and the emphases are not identical, but the time zones during which the transitions occur and the tasks that are considered crucial are not very different. Gould believes that in the fifties or thereabouts, a person's life becomes more serene than during the earlier, uncomfortable mid-life years. For Gould, it is possible to appear to be in one time zone but really, inwardly, to be in another.

Vaillant is another theorist carrying out studies in adult development. He studied college age men considered to be relatively free of mental health problems. Vaillant's theory, similar to the others, deals with development of the life cycle. He notes how the patterns and rhythms of the life cycle are geared to career planning. Self-exploration plays a major role. Like Levinson, he gives the mid-life crisis a prominent position in his theory, but Vaillant believes that examples of that crisis are more often seen in the clinic than in the world at large.

A Different View

Stage theorists see the process of development as one of continually completing new tasks or coping with new crises. They do not provide an overview of what is accomplished by aging, of what life is really like in old age. Butler, however, does provide such an overview, making the following points:

First, old age is the only period in life in which the future is less important than it had been; the present is what matters. Thus, there is a change in the sense of time. The quality of present time is more important than how much of it one has left. Older people can fully experience the now.

Second, old age is the only time when a person can experience a sense of the entire life cycle. There is an accumulation of factual knowledge; there is a sense of experience. These broad, wisdom-giving experiences can only come with age. They make resolutions of personal problems more possible and make for a good source of advice to others. Old people can be good counselors, but, unfortunately, they are not always seen as such.

Old people are attached to familiar objects of their past and value them. Objects such as home, pets, scrapbooks, and keepsakes provide a sense of comfort and continuity with the past. The old are the work-a-day historians; they are good reference sources. Not only do they want to keep a continuity with the past, but they also want to leave a legacy for the future. They want to pass on power, unless they are so fixated on themselves that they cannot. The old feel fulfilled if they can do all of these things while at the same time exercising their capacity for growth. Growth is possible at any age.

PERSONALITY

Types of People

Whether or not adult stage theories are valuable in understanding human personality development, they have provoked much interest and thought. One might expect, therefore, that they have had much influence on research in personality development, but they have not. Levinson's, Gould's, and Vaillant's stage theories may be too new to have generated much research, but Erikson's theory has been around long enough. However, only a few personality studies seem to be related to it.

In one study bearing on the Erikson theory, two groups of older people were selected, one consisting of persons high in the acceptance of aging and the other low in acceptance. Among those low in acceptance, some elderly were found to be aggressive, blaming each other for their miseries. Some were full of despair; they were self-haters. It seemed that they represented what Erikson suggested would be the fate of people not meeting the eighth stage of crisis in a satisfactory manner.

Those who accepted aging, however, did not have the fatalistic quality Erikson implied. They were of three types. One type was people who seemed to enjoy life and were pleased with what they were doing at the moment. Another type was those who enjoyed relaxation and not having to work. A third type was people who tried to keep active to defend themselves against old age. All of these types were satisfied people.

A later study by different investigators also described several personality types and had several points in common with the earlier study. The dissatisfied felt they were failures and feared that they would become dependent. Some had inferiority feelings, others suffered self-doubt, others lacked a clear concept of a role for themselves. They were fearful and suspicious. Those who were satisfied had self-identity, and were competent and socially perceptive. As in the first study, some kept active just to keep from falling prey to the effects of aging.

Characteristic Trends

Describing older people in the manner used above does not tell us much about personality changes over time. It simply describes how old people are seen at the time of the study. To really see how people change, they need to be studied longitudinally, that is, during at least two points in time.

Longitudinal Studies. It seems that there are only two pub-lished longitudinal studies reporting on personality changes. In one, Douglas and Arenberg tested men of a wide age range on two occasions, seven years apart. Their test measured ten traits; they found, not surprisingly, that after age 50 the pace of activity decreases. They also found a decrease in liking activity that is impulsive. This might be regarded as a positive sign because impulsivity can get people into trouble. The investigators also found that with time the men became less masculine. They did not become feminine, they just did not seem to need to express themselves in "macho" terms. (As we will see later, women seem to complement men in this way as they age.) There were other traits which were age related, but they could just as easily be attributed to sociocultural effects rather than to maturational age effects (and only maturational changes are compatible with stage theory thinking). There seemed to be a decline in agree-ableness, tolerance, cooperativeness, and trust in others in inter-personal relations.

The other longitudinal study was undertaken by Schaie and Parham. Here, too, people of a wide age range were tested twice, seven years apart. With age, men and women were seen to become more conventional and more alert to practical needs. They were less excitable and more accepting, probably making them easier to live with. Unlike the participants in the other study, age in these people seemed to increase their trust in others.

Cross-Sectional Studies. In the single comparisons of young and old during a single point in time, that is, in cross-sectional studies, a wide variety of traits seemed to be age related. There seems to be a decreased intensity and frequency of emotions, a decreased need for achievement, and a greater interest in conformity and self-control. Interest in self-control goes with the decrease in impulsivity that was found in the longitudinal research. Masculinity was again found to decrease.

Tests showed that older people were more introverted than younger ones. This checks with the idea that older people disengage, as described in Chapter 7. Older people were seen as less happy go lucky. They are often more depressed than younger people and often have reason to be since they are experiencing losses of various kinds.

Many older people are preoccupied with body functions and health; they become upset over it. If carried too far, they are labelled hypochondriacs. Women show this trait more than men.

Many old people seem rigid, but this rigidity is not so much a personality characteristic as it is a behavior tendency that appears when they are confronted with an inability to develop new solutions to problems that in the past were easily solved.

Other old people appear cautious but this too may not be a true characterization. It seems that many elderly prefer not to get involved in problem situations and merely look cautious when they are trying to avoid them. When forced into problem situations, however, they do not act differently from younger people. Older people are careful and try to avoid mistakes. This is a type of cautiousness that seems to be a generally positive trait. They seem to prefer a situation that is unambiguous; they seem to want certainty in their environment and are uncomfortable and often function poorly when there is little structure.

Different Sex Patterns

Sex Role Reversal. The decrease in masculine interests that aging men display appears to be matched by a corresponding change among women. Neugarten described an interesting study by her colleague, Gutmann, who studied aging in different societies and found similarities across the cultures. As men became elderly, they changed from active to passive in an effort to control their social environment and adapt to it. Women on the other hand, moved toward a more active, aggressive role. There was a reversal in the male-female patterns of young age.

A tentative and controversial explanation was offered to explain this sex reversal pattern. Until recently, at least, men and women had to establish different roles in early adulthood, especially in regard to childrearing. Women had to suppress aggressive impulses toward the children while men needed to encourage aggressive impulses in building a career. After children have grown and left the home, more natural impulses can be permitted. The woman can become aggressive and the man less so. The sexes become more similar; they become more as they had been before the children were born.

While this explanation may be subject to disagreement, the observation of reversal of sex roles has been noted through the years. It was noted in an earlier study of quite a different kind: Neugarten and Gutmann had people view a picture of an older man and an older woman alongside that of a younger man and a younger woman. They were asked to make up stories about the people in the picture. In the stories, the older man and older woman reversed roles in regard to who is the authority in the family. Middle-aged story tellers saw the older man as the authority figure, but older participants saw the older woman in the dominant role. The older woman, it seems, became more tolerant of their aggressive impulses while the older men became more tolerant of their dependence and ability to be giving and supportive.

Marking Time. There is little doubt that men and women put different emphases on home and family. One study found that women marked time by such events as getting married, having babies, and children's graduation from school. Men, on the other hand, marked time by events that occurred outside the home, often by occasions that relate to the job, as, for example, promotions and changes in positions.

An interesting thing happens to both men and women as they age. A point is reached where they mark off time differently than they did earlier in their life. Young people mark time by counting the years from birth; older people mark off time in terms of how much of it is left to them, e.g., how many more years until retirement, or how many more years they might live. Young people consider the past an anchor point, whereas old people look ahead to the end.

STABILITY WITH AGE

Many different personality traits of the old and young have been studied and a few changes over time have been described. However, while many traits seemed to differentiate old and young, many did not. For example, in the longitudinal study by Douglas and Arenberg where ten traits were measured, only five showed a change. They also carried out a cross-sectional analysis and five showed a change, but this could be attributed to cultural conditions, not age. Three traits showed no aging effect either cross-sectionally or longitudinally: sociability, emotional stability, and objectivity.

The same was observed in the longitudinal study by Schaie and Parham. They measured 19 personality traits and only six reflected a longitudinal age change. More traits were different among age groups cross-sectionally, but again, the difference could be due to cultural differences among the age groups. Five of the 19 traits showed no age difference either longitudinally or cross-sectionally. These investigators were so unimpressed with what they could identify as personality changes that they concluded that "stability within generations appears to be the rule."

Those age changes that have been identified do not seem to be major ones. Nothing very startling seems to happen in old age. The old are much like the young; life around them changes, so adjustments have to be made. A good guess of what kind of a person you will be when you are old is to examine yourself when you are still young.

REFERENCES

Botwinick, J. *Aging and Behavior.* Springer Publishing Co., New York, 1978. Chapters 5, 6, 7, 8 and 9.

Butler, R.N. *Why Survive? Being Old in America.* Harper and Row, New York, 1975.

Douglas, K. and Arenberg, D. "Age Changes, Cohort Differences, and Cultural Change on the Guilford-Zimmerman Temperament Survey." *Journal of Gerontology,* 1978, 33, 737-747.

Erikson, E.H. *Childhood and Society,* 2nd ed. W.W. Norton Co., New York, 1963.

Gould, R. *Transformations: Growth and Change in Adult Life.* Simon and Schuster, New York, 1976.

Kohlberg, L. "Stages and Aging in Moral Development." *The Gerontologist,* 1973, 13, 497-502.

Levinson, D.J. et al. *The Seasons of a Man's Life.* Ballantine Books, New York, 1978.

Neugarten, B.L. "Personality Changes in Adulthood." Master Lecture of the series on the Psychology of Aging, 86th Annual Convention of the American Psychological Association, 1978.

Neugarten, B.L., Crotty, W.F. and Tobin, S.S. "Personality Types in an Aged Population." *Personality in Middle and Late Life,* edited by B.L. Neugarten, et al. Atherton Press, New York, 1964.

Neugarten, B.L. and Gutmann, D.L. "Age-Sex Roles and Personality in Middle Age: A Thematic Apperception Study." *Psychological Monographs: General and Applied,* 1958, 17, Whole No. 470.

Reichard, S., Livson, P. and Peterson, P.G. *Aging and Personality.* John Wiley and Sons, Inc., New York, 1962.

Schaie, K.W. and Parham, I.A. "Stability of Adult Personality Traits: Fact or Fable?" *Journal of Personality and Social Psychology,* 1976, 34, 146-158.

Vaillant, G.E. *Adaptation to Life.* Little, Brown, New York, 1977.

Chapter 9

Those in Need of Special Help

Up to now we have been discussing normal aging. The main part of this chapter deals with those old people who, although not so very different from the others in many ways, have become so impaired mentally that they are regarded as abnormal or pathological. In mild forms such impairment is not always recognized as abnormal, but in severe forms the difference becomes readily apparent. When impairment is severe, institutionalization is required, either in a mental hospital, a total-care nursing home of the type discussed in Chapter 2, or some other custodial setting. It is possible, of course, for such a person to remain at home with the family, but such an arrangement is a drain on the family's emotions and time, as well as often threatening the family's continued peace and contentment.

PSYCHOSES

The major problem with mentally impaired people has to do with memory and thinking. They have trouble going from one place to another by themselves; they start out to do something but find it hard to finish, and to carry out even simple responsibilities is beyond them. In extreme cases, they may not recognize their loved ones. Only a small minority of older people are like this, but more have mild forms of this disability.

Mild forms do not make for any special problems if the social and economic context is compatible to the need. For example, the old woman who is forgetful, appears erratic and sometimes confused, but who has money and lives with a caring, understanding family can usually manage well. She may take a taxi to visit friends or go shopping or, if she is very wealthy, have her chauffeur take her around. On the other hand, if such a woman needs to work to maintain herself, or lives alone, she is in trouble. If this person has to take buses to go to one place or another, she may not be able to do it, especially if the trip involves transfers. In the case of the wealthy woman, her impairment may not even be seen as impairment. She may be regarded as a slightly eccentric, perhaps colorful, old person. In the case of the more needy woman, her mental status will be seen as pathological, and she will be brought to a doctor's attention. So much of what is known medically and what calls for medical diagnosis is a matter of social and economic circumstance. It is not often realized that both medical diagnoses of older patients and the recommendations based on them depend upon the social and economic background of the patient.

Temporary Decline

Changes in mental status vary from mild to severe and from temporary to permanent. The temporary changes can result from a variety of different causes, depression being one of them. Depression is common in many older people and often is not based on anything apparent. It is different from bereavement resulting from the loss of a loved one or from some other obvious reason. By and large, people get over this type of depression with the setback being short-term.

When grief is pronounced and continues beyond a reasonable time, or when there is depression for no apparent reason, it is said to be pathological. Such depressive psychosis is frequently accompanied by diminution in the ability to remember, think, learn, and act intelligently. These losses in cognitive behavior can be accompanied by disorganization, confusion, and, often, irrational and sometimes bizarre behavior. Such losses are recovered when the depression lifts, if there have been no physical changes in the brain. Diagnosis during the depressive period is difficult, because the cognitive symptoms are so similar in depression when there is organic brain change and when there is not.

Older people sometimes suffer nutritional deficiencies because they do not eat well. They do not take the trouble to prepare appetizing, wholesome meals, especially when they live alone. There may be metabolic problems. Such conditions can also make for cognitive deficiencies. When proper diet and bodily processes are restored, so are the cognitive skills.

Brain tumors or negative reactions to drugs and infections can make for behavior resembling organic brain changes. These too are lifted by a restoration to non-toxic, healthy conditions, if permanent debilitating organic change did not occur in the process.

Permanent Decline

Two Major Psychoses. There are two main types of organic brain conditions which give rise to disabilities and the behavior described above. They are very hard to tell apart: one gets progressively worse, and the other, while also downhill, has a more uneven course.

The process which is irreversible and progressively downward is called senile dementia of the Alzheimer type. About 50 percent of all old people suffering such cognitive deterioration have this psychosis. The cause of this difficulty is presumed to be progressive loss of brain cells. Along with diminution of cognitive skills go poor judgement, sloppy personal habits, and loss of interest. Previous personality traits—good and bad—may be exaggerated.

About 15 to 25 percent of those suffering from cognitive decline are thought to have cerebrovascular psychosis. Here the blood vessels in the brain either narrow (atherosclerosis) or harden (arteriosclerosis), which keeps an adequate blood supply from reaching the brain cells to nourish them. Thus, in both senile dementia and cerebrovascular psychosis, some brain cells are thought to be functioning inefficiently or not at all. Cerebrovascular psychosis, especially in the early stages, is often associated with dizziness and headaches. Very prominent in this disease is history of problems with heart or blood circulation. In fact, doctors take conditions such as high blood pressure and strokes into consideration when making the diagnosis.

There are other organic brain syndromes, but they constitute a minor percentage. For example, there is Wernicke-Korsakoff psychosis, which is associated with nutritional deficiencies of alcoholism. The symptoms of these other organic brain syndromes are in many ways similar to the two major ones and the diagnosis at least partly depends upon the history of the patient.

Is Psychosis Inevitable? Is it the fate of all older people, if they live long enough, to end up in such a sad state of cognitive loss and confusion? There are two opinions and one is affirmative. Those holding this opinion point to the fact that brain cell loss is continuous through life, but we have so many extra ones that it does not usually matter. A point is reached, however, when it does matter and reaching this point is inevitable if we live long enough. Further, the brains of severely deteriorated old people, when studied microscopically after death, show brain cell loss and a variety of tangles, plaques, and other nervous system changes. These are not different, the argument goes, from what is found in the brains of normal older people, except that in normal people there are fewer such changes.

The counter-argument maintains that there is normal aging and pathological aging, and the two processes are different. The large majority of older people does not suffer from psychosis, and to say that psychosis is inevitable, is misleading and damaging. Most scientists support this position. Whatever the answer, it is important to remember that most old people are in good control of their minds.

MENTAL HEALTH AND DAILY LIVING

Even though most old people are normal and do not suffer from psychoses, many have problems in daily living which may be painful; help is needed. This help is often not received. It is estimated that approximately 85 percent of those over 65 who could benefit from mental health services are not receiving them. Twelve to 22 percent of this age group display personality disorders but only two percent of the elderly are seen in psychiatric outpatient clinics. Professional workers such as psychiatrists, psychologists, and social workers tend not to be as interested in the old as in the young and are not as available to the elderly. Further, as a group, such professional workers have not received much training in service to the aged and lack appropriate information. Theories of personality and psychopathology are seldom concerned with the aged, and therapeutic techniques especially appropriate to them have not yet been developed.

Many older people, including those 85 percent who are in need of services and are not getting them, need help only in managing their lives: they do not need psychiatric help or drugs to alleviate anxiety. They need counseling as to what services are available and how they can obtain them. A good many of the elderly lack vital information, have no transportation to get help, have fears about being left alone when sick, and need nursing services at home. Many also need advice on money management, which could and should be made readily available but too often is not.

The major problem is that more services are needed and professional people need more training in the care of the aged.

There is another problem, also a major one. Old adults are not accustomed to seeking counseling or other mental health services. Behavioral therapy has a bad meaning for many of them. Unlike young people today, many of the elderly seem to consider those receiving mental health help as different, as "mental cases," and as "crazy." Many will not go for help even when it is available and they know where to get it. They, like the professional people, need to learn more about mental health services. They need to learn that it is all right to receive such help, as well as what kind of help is available.

REFERENCES

Botwinick, J. *Aging and Behavior.* Springer Publishing Co., New York, 1978. Chapter 13.

Butler, R.N. and Lewis, M.I. *Aging and Mental Health.* The C.V. Mosby Co., St. Louis, Mo., 1977. Chapter 5.

Cyrus-Lutz, C. and Gaitz, C.M. "Psychiatrists' Attitudes Toward the Aged and Aging." *The Gerontologist.* 1972, 12, 163-167.

Dye, C.J. "Psychologist's Role in the Provision of Mental Health Care for the Elderly." *Professional Psychology.* Feb. 1978, 9, 38-49.

Eisdorfer, C. and Cohen, D. "The Cognitively Impaired Elderly: Differential Diagnoses." *The Clinical Psychology of Aging.* edited by M. Storandt, I. Siegler, and M.F. Elias. Plenum Press, New York, 1978.

Ginsberg, A.B. and Goldstein, S.G. "Age Bias in Referral for Psychological Consultation." *Journal of Gerontology.* 1974, 29, 410-415.

Kramer, M., Taube, C.A. and Redick, R.W. "Patterns of Use of Psychiatric Facilities by the Aged: Past, Present, and Future." *The Psychology of Adult Development and Aging.* edited by C. Eisdorfer and M.P. Lawton. American Psychological Assn., Wash. D.C., 1973.

Lowenthal, M., Berkman, P.O. et al. *Aging and Mental Disorder in San Francisco.* Jossey-Bass, San Francisco, 1967.

Shanas, E., Townsend, P., Wedderburn, D., Milhoj, P., Friis, H. and Stehouwer, J. *Old People in Three Industrial Societies.* Routledge, London, 1968.

Terry, R.D. and Wisniewski, H.M. "Structural and Chemical Changes in the Aged Brain." *Aging.* Vol. 2, edited by S. Gershon and A. Raskin. Raven Press, New York, 1975.

Chapter 10

Contact with the Physical and Social World

We turn now to a very different aspect of aging but one that is important, nonetheless. We will consider how we make contact with things and people around us; we will discuss our sensory systems and how these change with age. We know the most about hearing and seeing, but little is known about taste, smell, pain, and touch. It is through our senses that we know what is around us; it is through them that we can interact with others. Those fortunate enough to have their senses intact, especially hearing and seeing, cannot begin to understand how difficult life can be without them.

Aging is associated with sensory loss and this alone could make life difficult. However, so much technical progress has been made that this loss becomes a problem only in extreme conditions. We have glasses to help us see better and hearing aids to help us hear better. These functions decline with age, but much of the sensory loss is correctable. What is not correctable makes the older person's relationship to his environment and his social relations difficult.

HEARING

Hearing Versus Seeing

People who have both sight and hearing tend to think of the ability to see as the more important of the two. Actually, total deafness seems to be a greater impairment than total blindness. The blind person can communicate with most other people more easily than the deaf person. The blind person can be a part of a social group and can listen to the radio or TV. Mobility is restricted but a social life is possible. The deaf person, on the other hand, must rely on other methods of social communication and most people with good hearing just do not know these methods.

Although relatively few old people are deaf or blind, just about all older people experience some loss of hearing and sight. The losses range from very minimal to appreciable. Typically, the older the person, the greater the loss. Even in instances where there is no total deafness or total blindness, hearing problems seem to be more incapacitating than visual problems. Two studies were carried out in which people over 60 were categorized in terms of their ability to see and hear. Those with hearing losses were found to be functioning at lower intellectual levels than those with better hearing. Not so those with seeing problems; they functioned on the same levels as those with better eyesight. It seems that it is harder to acquire information, develop skills, and correctly perceive what is going on when there is hearing loss than when there is visual loss.

A Special Kind of Loss

Among the best researched areas is hearing ability in relation to age. It is well documented that as people get older certain sounds are harder to hear. High pitched tones, such as those a soprano can reach, are progressively less audible for the elderly while those of a lower pitch, middle notes on the piano, for example, are easier to hear. Older people have difficulty with bass sounds, too, but it is mainly the high pitched tones—those of high frequency—that give old people problems.

This problem with high frequency is called *presbycusis*. Presbycusis tends to become apparent at about age 50 and gets progressively worse. The higher the frequency of the sound, the lower the age at which problems become apparent.

Speaking and Listening

Not only does presbycusis mean that the older person has difficulty with high frequency sounds, it also means that he has difficulty discriminating among such sounds. The consonants in speech are of a higher frequency than vowels. Thus older people have more trouble hearing correctly whether the spoken word was "*b*at" or "*c*at" than whether it was "f*u*n" or "f*a*n." Again, it is during the fifties that speech confusions become apparent and get worse.

Speech Perception. This suggests that speech perception, or language communication, gets impaired in old age. What is more, the faster the speech, the more the words are run together, the more is speech perception impaired. The rate of information processing also slows with age. Old people, man and wife, for example, may have trouble communicating with one another if presbycusis is severe. Social interactions become limited and loneliness can set in even when in the company of others.

The older person with such hearing problems may be at the greatest disadvantage when teenagers who speak quickly and use words that are unfamiliar are present. This tends to be more true of girls than boys, because girls' voices are higher pitched.

Older people may also have another problem in social interaction. They can have difficulty in separating speech sounds from background noises. If a noisy air conditioner or loud traffic sounds accompany an ongoing discussion, the older person may have more difficulty hearing. This applies to everyone, but it is worse when speech perception is faulty.

Helping the Older Person. The prescription for speaking with older people with presbycusis is to (1) speak slowly and pronounce words carefully; (2) avoid unfamiliar words, for example, slang, which is not part of the old person's vocabulary; (3) avoid distracting background sounds when possible; (4) speak louder than usual but not too loudly. Louder speech helps, but if it is too loud it makes things worse. It annoys others and makes continuous conversation difficult; and (5) have the listener look at you. This focuses attention and minimizes distraction. Focusing on the speaker's lips sometimes helps since the word-sounds are highlighted by how the lips form them.

Not every old person has difficulty communicating, of course. Difficulties are caused only by extreme problems; most old people have slight, but not extreme hearing problems. Some hearing problems can be helped by hearing aids, but they are expensive and not as easily tailored to an individual's need as are eye glasses. Hearing aids are of two general kinds. Most raise the loudness of all sounds so that problems with high frequency are aided because they become easier to hear. A minority of hearing aids increase the loudness of only those sounds with which there is difficulty. This kind is more expensive because the sounds that need increasing vary from person to person and therefore necessitate a more technically complex instrument.

Age Versus Environment

Presbycusis is more pronounced among men than women. Since it is known that loud sounds damage hearing, it has been suggested that men are more prone to presbycusis because of "noise pollution." It is thought that men are subject to greater noise pollution than women because their jobs more often entail such hazards. If this is true, we can expect that as women begin to do more and more of the same kind of work as men, their hearing will become equally impaired when they reach age 50 and above.

An interesting series of studies has lent this thinking credence. These studies suggest that it is not age that makes for presbycusis but the many years of living in environments which slowly but ultimately damage hearing mechanisms. A group of scientists went to an area in Africa where environmental noise levels were very low. They found very little presbycusis with advancing age. The combination of age and environmental damage may be what impairs hearing.

Cautiousness and Hearing Loss

The old hearing tests (audiological tests) were very simple. Different frequencies or pitches of sounds were presented and the person taking the tests was asked whether he heard the particular sound frequency. If the person said no, the loudness level was increased until he or she said something like "Yes, I hear it now."

Several studies showed that, for some reason, older people were less inclined than younger people to indicate they heard the sound when it was so low that they were not sure. Younger people were more inclined to say yes even when they were not sure. In other words, older people tested with such procedures might come out looking more impaired than they really were because of this caution.

These simple audiological procedures are being replaced by newer methods of testing. Many, if not most, hearing tests today are based on the newer method, called *signal detection.* This method takes into consideration the individual's personality characteristic, i.e. conservatism. (Signal detection is too complicated to describe here, but for a more detailed description, see Green and Swets.)

SEEING

When people talk about seeing they usually mean how clear things look and how much detail can be spotted. Scientists, however, mean this and more.

Visual Acuity

What most people mean when they talk about seeing ability, scientists call *visual acuity*. This is measured by eye tests where different letters or numbers have to be read from a given distance and reported aloud. There are different forms of this test, all of them having in common the reporting of the smallest letter or number that can be read correctly at a given distance.

If the normal eye can see numbers or letters at 20 feet and the person taking the test cannot, he is given progressively larger numbers or letters until he can see them well. These larger items are translated into viewing distance. For example, if the normal eye can see the larger items at 40 feet while the person taking the test sees them only at 20 feet, he is said to have 20/40 vision. The top number is a reference point of what good, normal vision is, the bottom number tells how far off from normal vision he is. The higher the bottom number the worse the visual acuity.

Up to age 40 or 50, little change in visual acuity is noted, but in subsequent years decline sets in. By age 70, most people notice that their eyesight is not what it used to be. This is no big problem, however, because correction with eye glasses is a simple matter unless certain specific visual defects arise. For example, the back of the eye, called the retina, has blood vessels on it. If these vessels become arteriosclerotic, correction is difficult. There are other problems, but it is important to remember that in most instances the diminution of visual acuity is not a difficult thing to correct.

Vision for Reading

In addition to loss in visual acuity with advancing age, which means less ability to see things well at a distance, there is also a loss in the ability to see objects up close, such as printed words in newspapers. The lens of the eye loses its elasticity and people become farsighted. *Accommodation* is said to be impaired.

This happens gradually; what most people do not realize is that the decline actually begins in childhood but is so gradual that it is not until age 40 to 45 that people begin noticing it. When it becomes noticeable, it is called *presbyopia*. Like visual acuity, presbyopia is not difficult to correct with glasses. Most older people need correction for both visual acuity and presbyopia; they can get bifocals.

Illumination

Everyone knows that if there is insufficient light, it is hard to see; this applies particularly to the elderly because they need more light to see well. Bringing up the *level of illumination* helps everyone, but it helps the old more. One reason for this, it is believed, is that the pupil of the eye gets smaller with age. Light goes through the pupil to the back of the eye. Since smaller pupils let less light through, the old need more illumination to get the same amount of light as the young do.

There are many situations where the need for more illumination is apparent and where problems can arise. For example, driving at night may be dangerous. Most older people should avoid wearing sunglasses when driving at dusk. Another feature regarding illumination levels is *dark adaptation*, that is, how long it takes a person to see well in relative darkness after having been in light, and how good sight is in the dark. It is obvious from what has already been said that aging and driving in the dark are not compatible. It is not clear whether age is related to quickness in dark adaptation, but it is clear that driving in the dark may be even more dangerous following the transition from light to dark. Depth perception also is impaired in later life and this impairment is made worse when there is little illumination.

Glare and Cataracts

Some older people suffer from glare. One way to be more comfortable is to reduce the level of illumination, cutting down the glare, but this leads to a conflict. While the old need more illumination to see well they may experience glare with it. As one investigator put it, typical lighting in most places is geared to the young eye. It would be ideal for the elderly if it were geared to the older eye. Perhaps, a fair solution is to put the lighting, in public places at least, at levels of illumination between that best suited for the young and for the old.

The glare from which some old people suffer is caused by a change in the lens of the eye. About 20 to 25 percent of people over 70 suffer from their lenses becoming cloudy and yellowish. Light rays passing through the pupil get scattered by the cloudy lens instead of going directly to the retina. The scattering of light makes for the glare.

When the clouding and yellowing of the lens becomes severe, sight is much impaired. To help this condition, the lens is removed surgically in a cataract operation. This has become a very commonplace procedure which greatly increases a person's ability to see. Glasses or contact lenses must then be used as a replacement for the natural lens that has been removed. More and more, lenses are surgically implanted.

One negative feature of cataract removal is that things look bigger than they are afterwards, but there is also an added benefit. With cataracts, the scattering of light rays makes for glare. Maybe this is the reason so many of the elderly seem to prefer dark sitting rooms to bright, sunny ones. When the opaque lens, the cataract, is removed, however, glare problems diminish or disappear altogether.

Color Vision

Colors are perceived differently by the old and the young. Some colors are about as clear and vivid and as easily told apart by old people as they are by younger ones, while some other colors are not. The yellowing of the lens mentioned above filters the light as it enters the eye so that blues and violets become more nearly similar in appearance for older people. On the other side of the color spectrum, the yellows and reds appear to the elderly more nearly as they appear to younger people.

To sum up, old people may have trouble telling blues, blue-greens, and violets apart, while reds, oranges, and yellows are easily differentiated. The difficulty in discriminating among the blues, greens, and violets suggests that color coding of home appliances, power tools, and the like should be such that only one of the colors in the first group is used. Pills prescribed for older people by doctors to be taken morning, noon, and evening should be color coded for easy discrimination. To prescribe blue pills for the morning and green pills for later in the day is not a good idea.

OTHER SENSES

We do not know much about the other senses and their relation to age. The reason is that it is much more difficult to do research on them.

Taste and smell go together, as seen by the lack of taste of foods when one's nose is clogged. Some studies show a decline of taste sensitivity with advancing age but a few do not. Studies showing decline have placed its apparent start in the late fifties. Taste ability depends on several factors. Smoking seems to diminish the ability to taste, and attitudes toward food and eating also play an important role.

There is even less research on the sense of smell and age, and what does exist is not clear. One study showed no decline with age among unusually superior people.

There is much clinical evidence to the effect that old people do not feel pain as intensely as do young people. Severe internal diseases of the aged do not seem nearly as painful to them as they would to younger adults. Minor surgery can often be performed on old people without inflicting severe pain. Despite this, subjective sensory complaints are very common in old age.

Such clinical evidence is only rarely supported by research evidence. Some studies show a lessening in pain sensitivity with age and some do not. Up to age 60, little, if any, change is observed. After age 60, some studies report a decline.

The sense of touch, like that of pain, varies with the part of the body stimulated. There seems to be even less research on touch than on pain. What data are available suggest that touch sensitivity remains the same until about 50 to 55, when some decline has been detected.

Overall, studies of the different senses show a reduction in sensitivity with age, smell being a possible exception. In general, the sensory losses are minor until the fifties, when they become more evident. In any case, these declines present a real problem for the older person only when they are extreme. In the case of vision and hearing, help is often possible even when the problem is extreme.

REFERENCES

Botwinick, J. *Aging and Behavior.* Springer Publishing Co., New York, 1978. Chapters 10 and 11.

Corso, J.F. "Auditory Perception and Communication." *Handbook of the Psychology of Aging,* edited by J.E. Birren and K.W. Schaie. Van Nostrand Reinhold Co., New York, 1977.

Fozard, J.L., Wolf, E., Bell, B., McFarland, R.A. and Podolsky, S. "Visual Perception and Communication." *Handbook of the Psychology of Aging,* edited by J.E. Birren and K.W. Schaie. Van Nostrand Reinhold Co., New York, 1977.

Green, D.M. and Swets, J.A. *Signal Detection Theory and Psychophysics.* John Wiley, New York, 1966.

Rosen, S., Bergman, M., Plester, D., El-Mofty, E. and Sath, M. "Presbycusis Study of a Relatively Noise-free Population in the Sudan." *Annals of Otology,* 1962, 71, 727-743.

Chapter 11

Learning, Memory, and Information Processing

No one is surprised by the information that hearing and seeing get worse with old age and few would be surprised if told that learning and memory abilities decline. The fact is, they do and they do not, depending on the kind of learning and memory we are talking about.

Learning and memory seem to mean different things and yet, when it comes to measuring these abilities in the laboratory, as we have to in order to understand them, it is nearly impossible to tell them apart. To test for learning, we have to ask questions about what has been learned, and that is memory. For example, a test instruction might read something like this: "Here is a list of words; learn them. Later, I will test you to see what you learned." This is a test of recall of what has been learned. Recall is a type of memory.

On the other hand, to test for memory, something has to have been learned. Obviously, there cannot be a memory of nothing learned. Learning and memory are one and the same process.

Given the oneness of learning and memory, it is strange that American experimental psychology was in the 1940s and 1950s basically a psychology of learning, in the 1960s a psychology of memory, and in the 1970s an extension of it, called information processing. The core of information processing is not much different from the core of psychology—there is information, there is its perception and acquisition, there is its retention, and there is its use. Before the information can be used, something has to be done with it. The user has to process the information and work on it to learn. How people work on information to learn and retain it is a major concern of psychologists.

LEARNING

Learning is acquisition of information or skill and memory is its retention. Learning and memory, as indicated, are one and the same process: something has to be put in memory storage (learning) and that something has to be recalled and used (memory). Psychologists have taken to using the words *encoding* and *retrieval* for these processes. Information has to be put in some other form than it is to place it in *storage*. A list of words, for example, cannot be put in mind as is. The words have to be encoded in some way. Once encoded, once in mind, they have to be retrieved. We have so much information in mind that retrieval mechanisms have to be able to select the wanted information only. Encoding and retrieval functions constitute a major part of intellectual life.

Since the processing of information starts with acquisition or encoding, we might start with the question of how older people fare in this kind of work in comparison with younger people. In other words, does learning ability decline with age?

Pacing

This question sounds easy to answer but is not because different conditions of learning and different conditions of showing what has been learned give different results. For example, it makes a difference whether information comes in a rapid sequence or whether it comes slowly. It makes a difference also whether the learner has to show what has been learned quickly or whether he can take his time about it. In other words, the pacing, or speed of both information input and response utilization, is important in the learning performances of older people.

When information sequences are paced quickly, when one item of information comes soon after another, as it might on some jobs—for a flight controller in a busy airport, for example—the elderly are much disadvantaged. Similarly, when the information must be responded to quickly, the elderly are at a disadvantage. However, when information input is slow or, better still, when the person can control the information input rate—as in learning a list of grocery items—the older person shows up well. He may not show up as well as the young person, but he certainly is not far behind. Much of what is seen as a learning deficit in old age is a deficit in the speed of processing and utilizing information. Other than that, learning appears to hold up relatively well with advancing age.

Type of Information

Type of Encoding. Learning holds up will with age but more so for some kind of information than for another. Information that can be encoded or learned on the basis of its physical properties will be no harder to learn for the old than the young. For example, learning which colors go together would probably be as easy for one age group as another. The physical property of color is attended to and compared with others. Similarly, information that is based on the sound of things would tend also to be learned well by the aged. A spoken string of telephone numbers following the exchange number might make for a fleeting sound or resonance in the ear. These numbers would be learned about as well by the old as the young.

When information requires processing that goes beyond

the physical or sound (phonemic) aspects, when it involves at-taching meaning to the information or abstracting parts of it and integrating it with other information, it is said to involve deep-level processing and semantic elaboration. This kind of learning seems to decline with age, but it is important to note that learning is not an all or nothing affair. If the learning is less than complete, it can be completed with more deep-level process-ing. This can be speeded up with the use of learning and mem-ory aids, which will be discussed later.

Meaningfulness of Information. The foregoing suggests what is obvious: the more meaningful the information, the bet-ter it can be organized and integrated, and the more quickly it can be learned. Paradoxically, and contrary to common opinion, the more meaningful the information, the harder it is for the older person to learn it relative to the younger person. The key phrase here is "relative." Actually, meaningful material is more easily learned by all people, old and young, than meaningless, irrelevant information. However, if the meaningful information is difficult, and elaborative processing is required, young people, on the average, do this better than old people. Old people can learn meaningful information better than information that has no relevance to them, but they do not benefit from the meaning-ful aspect of the information as much as do younger people.

It is crucial to note that so far nothing has been said of past experience or of individual differences in learning and memory. Later, we will see that the old have as much or more information as the young, because their information goes further back. The use of what is learned is often more important than how much was learned, and there is no reason to believe that in this regard, the elderly need to take a back seat to the young. Wisdom based on experience can be found only among the elderly. As for indi-vidual differences, no study was ever conducted where some older people did not learn more than some younger ones. Very few studies have dealt with the wise use of information.

Aids to Learning and Memory

Since learning and memory "is" work, there are ways to make the work, the processing of information, effective. Work does not mean that the activity is unpleasant. It could be pleasant or otherwise, but learning and memory are not passive affairs. If the work is fun, it does not feel like work, but it is, nevertheless. *Mnemonic devices* aid learning-memory; they can help everyone, often the old more than the young.

First, whatever the information is that needs to be learned, the older person should try to visualize it in a different form. If it is a written word, for example, he should try to picture it in a three-dimensional, nonverbal form. Second, the information should be associated with something else, even if it is silly. Sometimes, the sillier the better. For example, if a shopping list is to be learned, the person can picture placing the food items in the pantry, or, if he so wishes, on the nose of a giraffe.

Another learning-memory device is to categorize the information. Put all things together that go together naturally—all the meat items, all the fruits, and so on. If the items do not go together naturally, make up something, even if it is an artificial grouping—all things that are especially tasty, for example.

Integrate knowledge with what you already know. President Kennedy was assassinated, so was his brother, so was Dr. Martin Luther King; there was an angry period of cultural change.

If numbers are to be remembered, it is better to hear them. The older person would do well to have someone read the numbers aloud to him. On the other hand, written prose is best retained by individual reading.

When possible, cues should be provided for recall. The cues should be given freely and not begrudgingly. Have the older person make notes for himself, if he can. Note-taking is a good technique but, for some reason, many older people do not do it or, if they do, they do not refer to the notes in a way that is help-ful. The older learner, like everyone else, likes to be commended and not reproved. Praise may help; reproof will likely make un-stable skills worse.

MEMORY AND INFORMATION PROCESSING

If learning and memory are considered one, if they are aspects of information processing, then, having discussed learn-ing, we have in a sense also discussed memory. This is largely true, but not completely. In discussing learning, information encoding was emphasized, but not information retrieval. The study of memory emphasizes different qualities than learning.

Types of Memory Versus Extent of Elaboration

There are two opposing concepts regarding learning and memory. The one presented here is that learning and memory are as good and long-term as the depth of processing. The great-er the elaboration of the information; that is, the more the ma-terial has been worked on, integrated with other information, and given meaning, the better the retention. Some types of in-formation lend themselves to deeper processing and more elab-oration than others and this is the type of information that can be retained longer. The other concept is that it is not a matter of different levels of information processing but of different kinds of memory. As disparate as these two concepts might appear, they seem to point to similar matters in regard to aging.

Primary Memory. There are at least two types of memory processes, or at least two major levels of processing. One is a very temporary, or short-term, memory, called *primary memory.*

It is not the kind we usually mean when we think of memory, but it is memory nevertheless. It is the kind of memory that is acquired by shallow processing of information, based on the physical or phonemic character. The recall of a few telephone numbers is primary memory.

Primary memory is fleeting. It does not last long unless the information is rehearsed or otherwise processed. Someone will call out the numbers or you will look them up in a phone book, and you will rush to the phone to dial. You may get all the numbers dialed, but it is likely that you will not remember them afterward. You are not likely to get all the numbers dialed if, between looking them up and getting to the phone, someone calls you or interrupts you in some way. The numbers are just circulating in mind, so to speak, and not part of permanent memory storage. The interruption knocks them out of the circulating process.

Primary memory, therefore, is memory of the present, of the "psychological now." It is an important type of memory because without it, speech communication would not be possible. We need to have words circulating in mind to attach them to what is coming next. Without primary memory, life would be an ever changing confusion with nothing present to hold. Age groups do not differ in primary memory or they differ only marginally. This is fortunate because with impaired primary memory there would be a most impaired present.

Primary memory is limited in size. Very few items of information can be circulated in mind at one time, perhaps only four or five. If more information is needed, or if the information in primary memory is needed for long-term use, it must be transferred to a long-term store. The information needs to be processed more deeply to transfer it to secondary memory.

Secondary Memory. This is more nearly what people think of when they think of memory. Unlike primary memory, which is short-lived and involves only a few items, *secondary memory* involves limitless amounts of information and is longer lived.

The length or duration of secondary memory is a matter of the depth of processing and the extent of the elaboration.

The memory can be permanent, for as long as the person lives. There can be thousands and thousands of memories filed away in the storage system. Secondary memory information is to be used now and in the future, as needed.

How does secondary memory hold up with aging? There are two dimensions to secondary memory storage: getting the information in storage in the first place and keeping the information there in the second. Getting the information in is a matter of encoding, processing, elaborating. As already indicated, this ability seems to decline with age. As to keeping the information in storage, this does not seem to be a problem for the old. They have a large fund of information and thus retain it for years on end. Some studies show that their stores of old memories are no smaller than those of younger people. They might even be larger because of their many years of experience.

This is why it is often said that the ability to retain old memories holds up well with age but the ability to retain new memories does not. Here is where the two concepts regarding memory are clearly different. One view is that old and new memory retrieval involves two different processes, different types of memory banks. The other view is that the storage mechanism is the same in both, the only difference being the depth of processing and the elaboration. According to this view, very old memories are well maintained in late life because they have been well processed earlier in life. The first view distinguishes between secondary and a long-term, *tertiary memory*; the other view makes no distinction and considers it all secondary memory.

To sum up, aging brings about encoding difficulties for many but leaves primary memory intact. Secondary memory is impaired to the extent that deep processing is involved, but old, long-term memories can last forever.

Measuring Memory

There are two basic ways of measuring memory. One involves the task of *recall*. For example, the investigator may ask, "Who was the third President of the United States?" If the information is in memory storage, in the memory bin, it must be retrieved. Memory must be searched and the information, Thomas Jefferson, retrieved. If the information was never in storage or retrieval is not working well, the correct answer cannot be given. The investigator does not know whether it never was in storage or whether the retrieval functions are deficient, but he knows that at least one of the two alternatives must apply.

Another way to measure memory is by multiple choice tests. "Who was the third President of the United States, Johnson, Jackson, or Jefferson?" Here, help is available and, if the information was ever in storage, it can be matched with the different alternatives. The greater the number of alternatives, the harder the task, because more information needs to be examined and differentiated. The more similar the alternate choices, the harder it is to differentiate among them. Instead of "Johnson, Jackson, and Jefferson," a choice among "Eisenhower, Kennedy, and Jefferson" would be easier. The multiple choice test is said to measure *recognition memory.*

As indicated, increasing age is associated with some difficulty in the ability to recall newly acquired information. The problem could rest with encoding; that is, placing the information in storage, or it could rest with keeping the information in storage. Using the analogy of a memory bin, it may be that the bin is defective or leaky. In either case, it would be said that the problem rests with storage mechanisms. On the other hand, the problem may be with retrieval functions. Recent studies show that recall of very old information is no worse among the old than the young, or, at least, not nearly as much of a problem as the recall of new memory. This suggests, therefore, that neither a defective bin nor a defective retrieval system seems to be the answer. This leaves encoding or learning as the answer, suggesting again that the elderly tend not to process information as deeply as the young.

While cross-sectional studies show less recall of new information with age, they show only little decline in recognition memory, if there is a decline at all. There are two views about explaining this difference in age pattern between recall and recognition memory. One view is that the two processes—recall and recognition—are different. Recall involves search and retrieval from memory, but recognition does not involve retrieval. All that is required is to match the information in storage with information in the environment; for example, matching the information. Thomas Jefferson, with the correct test item alternative. A search and match is required, but not a search and retrieval.

The other view is that recall and recognition are one and the same process, both involving retrieval. Retrieval requires processing of information just as does encoding. Recognition memory is easier than recall memory, particularly for the older person, simply because a cue or hint is given during retrieval processing. It will be recalled that providing a cue or hint is one of the aids or mnemonic devices which often helps the older person in his search for information in his memory store.

THE OMISSION ERROR

In a wide array of different contexts—in learning and memory studies, in perception studies, and in other kinds of studies—the older subject tends to make a characteristic error: he fails to respond. He gets marked wrong for not responding when asked to recall the information. Often, he gets more marks of wrong for not responding than for giving incorrect information. It seems as if the older person chooses not to respond, not to answer the question when he is unsure as well as when he does not know the answer. This is called the *omission error*. Even with instructions to guess, even when encouraged to respond quickly and not to deliberate or worry about being wrong, the inclination of the older person to make the omission error is strong. This has been interpreted in one study as a feeling of inadequacy on the part of the older people, and a wish to avoid this feeling as much as possible.

Lack of confidence seems to be the reason for this not responding, this fear of failing. A study was carried out based on this concept. It was a study of paired-associate learning. New associations had to be learned—associations such as "house-river," "book-tree," and so on. Among all learning tasks this type of paired-associate may be hardest for older people.

The typical pattern in such studies is to reward correct responses and not incorrect ones. Animal trainers even punish wrong responses and sometimes, parents, teachers, and therapists punish wrong responses, too. However, punishment often makes for negative by-products.

In this paired-associate study, the investigators started with the notions (1) that many older people make the omission error and (2) that unless responses are given, learning and memory performances are poor.

Accordingly, all responses made by older subjects, right or wrong, were rewarded, but the correct responses were given a greater reward than the wrong ones. The idea was to get the older people to make a response, be wrong if they must, but not to commit the omission error.

The results showed that the elderly who got rewards for both correct and incorrect responses learned quicker and better than those participants who were rewarded in the traditional way of rewarding only correct responses. These data showed that what may seem like a learning and memory deficit on the part of the elderly, may not be that at all. It may be a type of cautiousness, a fear to be wrong, or another kind of personality characteristic limiting the expression of what is learned.

An effort was made to repeat this study but the results were not the same. In fact, they were just the opposite: those who received monetary reward for all responses performed less well than those who were treated in the traditional way of being rewarded only when correct.

Why did the two studies yield such different results? Further investigation provided a plausible explanation. The second investigation compared older adults who were different in socioeconomic status from those in the first study. One group had more schooling and higher level jobs than the other group. It was the group with a higher socioecomonic status that performed better with reward for only correct recall. The poorer group performed better with monetary reward for all responses. The suggestion, therefore, is that the money may have meant more to the poorer old people and so, they were less inclined to make the omission error, the only kind of error that was not rewarded. The richer old people, on the other hand, may have not been as motivated to go against an ingrained inclination not to respond when uncertain of the answer.

Whether this explanation is correct, the fact remains that reducing the omission error improves learning and memory performances of some older people. This, then, is another mnemonic device. Encourage the older person to commit himself even if he is uncomfortable doing it.

Be supportive, non-punitive, rewarding, and encourage responding. Make it clear that making a mistake and being wrong is not tragedy. We all do it.

REFERENCES

Botwinick, J. *Aging and Behavior*, Springer Publishing Co., New York, 1978. Chapters 15, 16, 17 and 18.

Botwinick, J. and Storandt, M. *Memory, Related Functions and Age.* Charles C. Thomas, Springfield, Il., 1974. Chapter 9.

Botwinick, J. and Storandt, M. "Recall and Recognition of Old Information in Relation to Age and Sex." *Journal of Gerontology,* 1980, 35, 70-76.

Craik, F.I.M. "Levels of Processing: A Framework for Memory Research." *Journal of Verbal Learning and Verbal Behavior.* 1972, 11, 671-684.

Craik, F.I.M. "Age Differences in Human Memory." *Handbook of the Psychology of Aging,* edited by J.E. Birren and K.W. Schaie. Van Nostrand Reinhold Co., New York, 1977.

Craik, F.I.M. and Simon, E. "Age Difference in Memory: The Roles of Attention and Depth of Processing." *New Directions in Memory and Aging: Proceedings of the George Talland Memorial Conference,* edited by L.W. Poon, J.L. Fozard, L.S. Cermak, D. Arenberg and L.W. Thompson. Erlbaum, Hillsdale, N.J., 1979.

Erber, J.T. "Age Differences in Recognition Memory." *Journal of Gerontology,* 1974, 29, 177-181.

Erber, J., Feely, C. and Botwinick, J. "Reward Conditions and Socioeconomic Status in the Learning of Older Adults." *Journal of Gerontology,* 1980, 35, 565-570.

Leech, S. and Witte, K.L. "Paired-Associate Learning in Elderly Adults as Related to Pacing and Incentive Conditions." *Developmental Psychology,* 1971, 5, 80.

Schonfield, D. and Robertson, E.A. "Memory Storage and Aging." *Canadian Journal of Psychology,* 1966, 20, 228-236.

Taub, H.A. "Mode of Presentation, Age, and Short-Term Memory." *Journal of Gerontology,* 1975, 30, 56-59.

Chapter 12

Intelligence

Nowhere in the study of aging is there as much controversy as in the area of intelligence. Perhaps the major reason for this is that we value intelligence so much more than other functions. If that is so, it reflects a misconception of what intelligence is, at least as psychologists measure it.

WHAT IS INTELLIGENCE?

It is strange that people do not seem to mind saying, "Oh, do I have a bad memory!" but one would not want to admit, "Oh, do I have a low intelligence!" Memory is part of intelligence as are other cognitive abilities. Intelligence is a combination of several different abilities, some more important for some things than others.

Ability Versus Innate Potential

An old definition of intelligence, given with tongue in cheek, is still a good definition even if it is not very informative. "Intelligence is what intelligence tests measure." This means that the tests may or may not measure meaningful samples of behavior and may or may not leave unmeasured other very important behaviors. The point is, however, that behavior is measured and nothing else.

No test can measure the innate, biological, or genetic potential of the brain—the concept that is often thought of as intelligence. Efforts are made to infer this under-the-skin concept of the innate potential of the brain but the fact remains that tests measure only samples of behavior and the rest is inference.

Further, this inference has to take into consideration cultural opportunities and background experiences, a very difficult and controversial thing to do. Therefore, many behavioral scientists maintain that all that intelligence tests measure is current abilities. These abilities change with experience; they are not fixed over the lifetime; they are learnable skills.

There is another view that is not concerned with genetics or the innate potential of intelligence, but is concerned with brain function as it is reflected in intelligence-test behavior. People with such interests are called *neuropsychologists*. They associate performances on certiain kinds of tests with the functioning of one part of the brain, and performances on other kinds of tests with other parts of the brain. Nothing is said about potential intelligence in the genetic sense, but even here the performances must be analyzed in the context of cultural opportunities and experience.

Different Kinds of Intelligence

The most widely used test of adult intelligence is the Wechsler Adult Intelligence Scale (WAIS). It has 11 subscales, each measuring a different kind of intelligence. The 11 scales are not totally different since performances on them are correlated to some extent, but in the main they are thought to measure different aspects of intelligence.

Partly for convenience, six of the 11 subtests are grouped

together and called the Verbal scales. The remaining five are grouped together and are called Performance scales. The fact is that performance is measured with each of the 11 scales and some minimum verbal skill is necessary for good performance on all of them. Overall, however, the six Verbal scales require more verbal ability than the others, and most of the Performance scales require hand manipulation skills which the others do not.

Another test commonly used, more for research than for clinical use, is the test of Primary Mental Abilities (PMA). This test also has several subscales. Based partly on the PMA and partly on many other tests, Horn and Cattell have called one kind of intelligence *crystallized* and another kind, *fluid* intelligence. Crystallized intelligence tests are more similar to the WAIS Verbal scales than the others, and the fluid intelligence tests are more similar to the Performance scales. Crystallized intelligence tests measure abilities thought to be dependent on past experiences, such as education and environmental influences. Fluid intelligence, on the other hand, is thought to be more related to the functioning of the central nervous system. Past learning is important, but not to the extent it is in crystallized intelligence.

There are other tests of adult intelligence, but the WAIS and PMA are the main ones, except perhaps for those used by the military. Most tests, however, have verbal and non-verbal parts.

Are the Tests Meaningful and Fair?

This question is part of the controversy. Intelligence tests have come under attack in recent years on the basis that what they measure is often not relevant to the purpose for which they are used. There is little argument that the tests are most appropriate for young, white middle-class people, and that they may be unfair to those not of the majority culture. It would certainly not be fair to use tests to assess potential rather than present ability. The tests may be suitable to assess what can be done now, accepting the fact that not everyone has had a background rich enough to sustain optimal intellectual growth. Given this, then, of what use are intelligence tests?

Intelligence or similar tests are typically given to predict performances in school or on the job. People are admitted to schools and offered jobs partly based on these test scores. Is this fair? It is, if the following two conditions are met: (1) test performance is really predictive of school or job success and (2) the tester considers the possibility of remedial work at school or on the job training. Often, the prediction of school or job success is poor, and when it is, use of the test is neither fair nor wise. To the extent the test is a good predictor, its use is meaningful. When it comes to the second condition, that of training and remedial work, we should remember that people whose backgrounds were inadequate to develop intellectually can often catch up with a little help. It would seem that the use of tests without consideration of such help is unfair.

Not everyone believes that traditional intelligence tests can be meaningfully used with older adults. Demming and Pressey, for example, asserted that tests used to measure intelligence of older people should deal with problems relevant to them. Traditional tests often involve items more relevant to children or very young adults. Accordingly, Demming and Pressey constructed a test comprising information items that were more related to the needs of adults. They reported results of a test based "on use of yellow pages in a telephone directory, on common legal terms, and on people to get to perform services needed in everyday life." With this test, they found a *rise* in scores in the middle and later years among the very same people who had shown a decline in their scores with the conventional tests. This again points to the importance of validating a test in reference to the purpose for which it is administered. Very much more research is needed to clarify the important factors which make a test relevant to older people as they live their lives, not as they are seen in the laboratory.

Tests are also used for research purposes to learn about people's skills and abilities. It is with these research endeavors that the present chapter is concerned.

AGE AND THE IQ

Just as some learning and memory abilities remain intact with age and some do not, so is it with intellectual abilities. Generally, the Verbal or crystallized intelligence test functions hold up well with age but the Performance or fluid functions do not. When the two are averaged they show a decline.

There is no controversy about the observation that older people have lower scores than younger people. There is controversy, however, about what this means, and about how meaningful is the cross-sectional research method (where two or more age groups are compared). Some people believe that this method does not tell the correct story, because associated with age are a lot of cultural or historical facts that also relate to intellectual ability. For example, the schooling and intellectual opportunities for persons reared in 1910 were different from those brought up in 1960. These factors can be more important than age. These critics therefore recommend that other research methods be used.

The WAIS IQ

Cross-sectional studies show an overall decline of test scores with age. In most tests of adult intelligence, the score a person gets is based only on the number of items answered correctly. This score is not an IQ score, although people often refer to it as such. Perhaps surprisingly, most tests of adult intelligence do not use IQ scores. In fact only one, the WAIS, does, but as indicated, this is the most widely used test of all.

The IQ consists of the test scores plus or minus a number of points based on age: points are taken off the scores of young people and are added to the scores of the old. Therefore, if a 25-year-old man and a 75-year-old man each have the same IQ, the actual performance of the older man is poorer than that of the younger. The thinking is that it is average or normal for old people to perform less well than young people on this test and the IQ is therefore constructed to reflect this "normal" process. In this way, if in a person's lifetime there is no change in test performance, the IQ will go up over the years.

An IQ of 100 is said to be average. To keep this average across the ages, 32 points are added to the performance scores of those aged 75 and over, none are added to those aged 45 to 54, and ten points are deducted from the scores of those aged 20 to 24.

Meaning of Decline

The IQ, with the addition and subtraction of age points, does not reflect decline with age but, as indicated, the actual test performance does. What does that mean? Does it mean that the old are not as smart as the young? Or that only the young should be given the top jobs? The answer is no.

First, we are discussing group and not individual scores. A given old person may score very highly in comparison to anyone, young or old. Age is a very poor predictor of intelligence test scores despite the general downward trend.

Second, as emphasized earlier, it is important to be sure to know the reason why a test is being given. For example, a poor score on a test may indicate that the person will not do very well in school; this is not an important concern for a 70-year-old. The test may not indicate anything with respect to continued good performance in carrying out the responsibilities of a top job.

Third, as already mentioned, a low score on an intelligence test may be as much a reflection of little education as anything else. Older people tend to have had less formal schooling than younger people and this could well be the basis of the lower scores on the part of older people. We really need tests that examine their everyday on the job or in the home skills.

Given this, it is well to recognize that intelligence is an essential ingredient for much successful behavior. Its assessment can be very useful. However, if used in the wrong way or for the wrong purposes, intelligence tests can be less than useful or even damaging. Tests of intelligence seem best suited for research and clinical purposes. To repeat what was said at the beginning of this chapter: intelligence tests measure ability developed to the present time but not native ability. Developed abilities can be developed further at any age.

MEASURING INTELLIGENCE

Classic Aging Pattern

It was said that crystallized test performances tend to be maintained well into late life but not fluid test performances. This pattern can be called the *classic aging* pattern. The test functions that decline with age sometimes are of perceptual-integrative abilities, often involving speed of response; sometimes they are analytical in nature. The Block Design subtest of the WAIS may be thought of as a fluid intelligence test: the person is given several blocks with colors on them. There are instructions to make specified designs based on the colors by proper placement of the blocks. Here is another example of a fluid intelligence test: "□ is to ◇ as T is to ____. Choose one: ⌐L ⊢ ⊣ ⌐ ." Such tasks are thought to reflect thinking ability relatively independent of past experiences and opportunities. On the other hand, the crystallized tests are clearly based on prior learning. Such tests deal with general information, vocabulary, and comprehension of things to do in social situations.

These latter types of tasks, therefore, are thought to measure what elderly people already know rather than what they can learn or deduce from the situation. The Verbal or crystallized tests are thought to measure the amount of knowledge a person has by measuring familiar ways of dealing with familiar materials. In contrast, the Performance or fluid tests tend to measure the handling of unfamiliar materials. The fluid tests require the processing of new information (see Chapter 11) and the application of solutions that are not already in memory. Elderly people are good in crystallized but not in fluid abilities. This classic aging pattern seems to be nearly universal; it exists in both white and black populations, men and women, and in hospital as well as community residents.

There is one group, however, where the pattern is hardly evident, if it is evident at all. In Chapter 9, organic psychoses of the aged were discussed. People suffering from such disorders show a decline in the Verbal or crystallized intelligence functions in addition to the fluid ones. The scores of both types of intelligence are depressed.

Educational Levels

There is little doubt that education is much more important than age in regard to how well a person performs on an intelligence test. This is true for both crystallized and fluid types of tests, even though the fluid tests are meant to be relatively free of background experiences. Given this, it is not surprising to find that older people perform less well than younger people in that they tend to have less formal education. The average 75-year-old in the United States has not gone to high school while the vast majority of young adults are high school graduates. This is an important consideration in evaluating the test scores of young and old.

To the psychologist Green it was so important as to raise

doubts about the whole age-intelligence picture. Green gave the WAIS to adults of a wide range of ages and found the usual classic aging pattern. But then, he did something different. He selected only those older people and those younger people who had achieved the same in level of education. In other words, he matched the age groups for education, and when he did this his results showed no age decline.

Should age groups be matched for educational level before being compared? There is no simple, straightforward answer. the 75-year-old high school graduate may be an especially bright person to have gone so far in school; few of his cohorts did. On the other hand, the 20-year-old high school student may be ordinary; it was easy and he or she was expected to graduate from high school. Is it meaningful to compare two such people, one especially bright and one ordinary? In one way we may be comparing two different types, and in the other we are closing our eyes to the fact that education plays a role in test scores and that older people do not have as much formal schooling as younger people.

Fatigue

People get tired in the course of taking tests and this fatigue can make the test taker perform less well than otherwise. One study showed that the aged get tired sooner than the young, a fact that can bring down their performances. Should only short tests be given when comparing old and young? Again, the answer is not simple or straightforward.

Since measured intelligence is ability, not something innate, is ability measured when fatigued not something worth considering? People get tired on jobs but still have to continue working. On the other hand, if the purpose of the test is to see what a person can do under optimum circumstances, a long fatiguing test is not a good idea.

Health

Several studies have shown that elderly people who are healthy score better on tests of intelligence than those who are not. Moreover, it is the fluid type of test more than the crystallized which reflects the difference between the healthy and the unhealthy.

Later, when discussing longitudinal research, we will see that older people who die relatively soon after having taken the test tend to have been the ones who scored poorly on it. Based on the reasonable assumption that in the main the deaths were due to sickness, and the sickness made for the poor test scores, several investigators have contended that age is not related to test performance, but that sickness in old age is.

Is this a reasonable contention? It is, but again the answer is complicated. How do we separate aging and sickness? A lot of old people suffer from a variety of health problems, mainly problems of the heart and blood vessels. Do we select only the very healthy to test? This is the same as selecting only elderly high school graduates for testing or older people who do not fatigue easily. Testing only the very healthy makes for an unusual old group, but again, if the purpose is to see what aging does when the old and young are matched, the contention may be credible.

There are other factors which affect performances; for instance, hearing loss, socioeconomic status, motivation and anxiety. These need to be evaluated when comparing age groups and the same type of difficult decisions need to be made. Hearing loss is related to relatively poor WAIS test scores; older people more than younger people suffer from such loss (see Chapter 10). Should old and young people be matched for hearing ability before comparing their test performances? The same line of reasoning has to be applied: It depends on the purpose of the comparison.

LONGITUDINAL RESEARCH

Longitudinal research, where the same people are tested several times over the years, can tell us about age changes, while cross-sectional research, where two or more age groups are compared during one period of time, can tell us about age differences. The problem with cross-sectional research, as already indicated, is that what may look like an age difference is really a cultural difference because older people were reared in different cultural eras than younger people.

Environmental Influences

There is a problem with longitudinal research also—what may seem like age changes may really be changes resulting from environmental influences occurring during the course of the study. For example, one biological study showed that lung functions improved longitudinally among middle-aged and older people. The investigators concluded, however, that the improvement was not an age change, but was due to the fact that the participants realized that cigarette smoking and lack of exercise was hurting them. Accordingly, many stopped smoking and started exercising and their lungs became stronger and worked better. In cross-sectional studies, age and culture get mixed up. In longitudinal studies, age and environmental influences get mixed up. Psychologists call the environmental influences *time-of-measurement effects*, the sociologists call them *period effects*.

Selective Dropout

Despite the environmental influences, longitudinal studies can come closer to telling us what happens with age than cross-sectional studies. In general, longitudinal studies tell us that the decline is smaller than the cross-sectional studies suggest and that it starts later. Otherwise, the classic aging pattern is the same.

There is a special problem with the longitudinal studies over and above environmental influences, however. As tests continue over the years, the lower-scoring people tend to drop out from the study and the higher-scoring ones tend to stay in. Thus, as the study continues, the sample of subjects remaining becomes increasingly biased. Mainly the intellectually superior are tested in the later stages of the study.

Among the low-scoring people who drop out, obviously, are those who have died. This phenomenon is called *terminal drop*. Many investigators have tried to predict death on the basis of terminal drop scores. The thinking here is that if scores drop appreciably over time, or if a score is so low as to suggest that a drop has taken place, the test taker is in danger of dying. This research is continuing today, but whether it will prove worthwhile in terms of uncovering the need for medical attention is still uncertain.

Age Changes

Given the bias of selective subject dropout, what is the life course of intellectual ability? Longitudinal research based on superior children shows that from about age 14 to about 29 there is an appreciable increase. From 29 to about 42 there is a further increase, both in the functions that hold up well into old age (Verbal) and those that do not (Performance). Further testing to age 50 and beyond again shows an increase, although in this segment the only tests given were of the type that examines abilities generally well maintained in later life.

These series of studies show continuing increases in intellectual ability from the teens to over 50. However, these studies were based on people who were intellectually superior, people well above the average. Longitudinal data of more ordinary people show either maintenance of function from young adulthood to middle age or, in some instances, a slight reduction.

The major longitudinal study was carried out by the psychologist Schaie and his associates. The study used the PMA test, examining people in their twenties through seventies. The major finding was no decline to the fifties, with some small decline afterwards. The different kinds of intellectual abilities showed different age patterns, some steeper in decline than others, some showing maintenance until very late in life.

Ability Levels

Do young people of high intellectual ability remain high when they turn old? This question has been asked in several studies that have different conclusions. Taking all those studies together, we can arrive at an answer, albeit a tentative one.

There is no way of knowing whether a young person's ability level will diminish a lot, a little, not at all, or even improve when he reaches old age. It seems likely that this is as true for the intellectually able as for the less able. What does seem predictable, however, is that while the precise amount of gains and losses is uncertain, those who start out relatively bright will end up relatively bright. In other words, a person who has a very high ability level when young and ends up less high when old still has a level that is higher than the average.

CONCLUSIONS

Tests of intelligence measure abilities already developed, not innate or biologically potential abilities. Therefore, intelligence is not a static ability, it can improve with training. In fact, education more than anything else, certainly more than age, determines how well a person does on such tests.

Intelligence is made up of a variety of abilities and so, intelligence tests include a variety of subtests. Some of these subtest scores decline with age, some more than others, but some do not lessen at all until very late in life. Verbal abilities based on general information and past experiences tend to hold up well with age, and often even improve with age. On the other hand, abilities based on new learning, novel situations, perceptual-integrative skills, are apt to decline. The declines tend to be small, and some do not start until the person is in his fifties or sixties, but some start before, especially if speed of response is involved.

Persons with high ability levels when young tend to keep relatively high levels when old, but it is not possible to predict for the individuals whether decline with age will be great, small, or not take place at all. There may even be an improvement with age.

Although decline and improvement cannot be predicted, there is reason to believe that from the extent of test score decline, or from an unusually low test score, the likelihood of death can be predicted, even if with great error. Such predictions, called terminal drop predictions, are currently being investigated. Most studies make an effort to predict death within the next five years. If such studies are successful, the subjects could be put on medical alert. Life styles could be changed and, perhaps, life prolonged.

From a practical viewpoint, when all is said and done, differences among people are more important than differences among age groups. Some older people perform at intellectual levels that are higher than those of some young people. Although there is a correlation between age and intellectual ability, the correlation is very small.

REFERENCES

Birren, J.E. and Morrison, D.F. "Analysis of the WAIS Subtests in Relation to Age and Education." *Journal of Gerontology*, 1961, 16, 363-369.
Botwinick, J. *Cognitive Processes in Maturity and Old Age.* Springer Publishing Co., New York, 1967. Chapters 1 and 2.
Botwinick, J. "Intellectual Abilities." *Handbook of the Psychology of Aging,*

edited by J.E. Birren and K.W. Schaie. Van Nostrand Reinhold Co., New York, 1977.

Botwinick, J. *Aging and Behavior.* Springer Publishing Co., New York, 1978. Chapter 13.

Botwinick, J. and Birren, J.E. "Differential Decline in the Wechsler-Bellevue Subtests in the Senile Psychoses." *Journal of Gerontology.* 1951, 6, 365-368.

Demming, J.A. and Pressey, S.L. "Tests 'Indigenous' to the Adult and Older Years." *Journal of Counseling Psychology.* 1957, 2, 144-148.

Doppelt, J.E., and Wallace, W.L. "Standardization of the Wechsler Adult Intelligence Scale for Older Persons." *Journal of Abnormal and Social Psychology.* 1955, 51, 312-330.

Eisdorfer, C., Busse, E.W. and Cohen, L.D. "The WAIS Performance of an Aged Sample: The Relationship Between Verbal and Performance IQs." *Journal of Gerontology.* 1959, 14, 197-201.

Granick, S., Kleben, M.H. and Weiss, A.D. "Relationships Between Hearing Loss and Cognition in Normally Hearing Aged Persons." *Journal of Gerontology.* 1976, 4, 434-440.

Green, R.F. "Age-Intelligence Relationship Between Ages Sixteen and Sixty-Four: A Rising Trend." *Developmental Psychology.* 1969, 1, 618-627.

Horn, J.L. and Cattell, R.B. "Age Differences in Primary Mental Ability Factors." *Journal of Gerontology.* 1966, 21, 210-220.

Riegel, K.F. and Riegel, R.M. "Development, Drop and Death." *Developmental Psychology.* 1972, 6, 306-319.

Schaie, K.W., and Labouvie-Vief, G. "Generational Versus Ontogenetic Components of Change in Adult Cognitive Behavior: A Fourteen-year-Cross-Sequential Study." *Developmental Psychology.* 1974, 10, 305-320.

Chapter 13

Problem Solving and Creativity

If some kinds of learning and memory abilities decline with age (see Chapter 11) and some kinds of intellectual abilities decline (see Chapter 12), we would expect some kinds of problem-solving skills to decline also. They do, but so much of what is known is based on artificial laboratory problems that we can hardly say anything about solving problems in real life, which older people seem to do well. In fact, almost all that we know about learning, memory, and intellectual skills as well as problem solving has this problem of artificiality. It is so much easier to carry out studies in the laboratory than in real life situations that the life situations have been left untested. For this reason we are limited in what is known about cognitive functioning in relation to age.

COGNITIVE FACTORS IN PROBLEM SOLVING

Intelligence

Levels of Intelligence. Several investigators have attempted to determine how important intelligence is to problem solving. A variety of studies taken together indicate a relationship between intelligence and problem solving, but one that is rather complex. First, as indicated in the previous chapter, there are two major groupings of intellectual ability. One grouping is needed for some problem-solving tasks and the other for other tasks. Second, intelligence test scores, even when related to problem-solving ability, do not begin to tell the whole story. It is clear that some minimum level of intellectual ability is needed to solve problems: to have more or less intellectual ability below this minimum level is of no consequence in problem solving because the level is not high enough to succeed. Studies show that at very high intellecutal levels, some people solve problems and others do not. Intelligence is necessary, therefore, to solve the problems, but it does not account for all that is required to be successful. The next few sections discuss the factors other than intelligence test scores that relate to problem-solving ability. Where the specific level of intelligence seems most important to problem solving is in the middle ranges of ability. The specific levels of intelligence which are required in problem solving depend on the difficulty level of the task.

Age Differences. Older people have the required intelligence to solve many laboratory tasks, but cross-sectional studies tend to show them as having less ability than the young. The psychologist Arenberg carried out the only longitudinal study in problem solving. He tested people between the ages of 24 and 87 and then tested them again, almost seven years later. There was very little age decline; only people aged over 70 showed any decline whatsoever over the seven-year period. Arenberg pointed out that all the people he tested were of superior intelligence and that their intelligence test levels were not related to their problem-solving scores. He also pointed out that the selective dropout over the seven-year period (see Chapter 12) may have accounted for the maintenance of the problem-solving ability into late age.

Memory

To the extent that solving a problem involves keeping information in mind while trying out possibilities, memory should be important in problem solving. Three different types of studies show this importance.

One study simply correlated problem-solving scores and short-term memory scores and found a positive relation. Since the older people displayed poorer memories, their problem-solving scores also were poorer.

Another study compared old people with memory difficulties to old people with no such difficulties. The no-difficulty group was superior in the problem-solving task.

A third study was constructive not only in demonstrating the role of memory in problem solving, but also in what might be done about it. In this study, information that the investigators provided was needed to solve the problems. The investigators varied the access to this information. The variation was from placing the information in front of the problem solver and showing it all, to keeping some of it out of view and thus imposing a burden on memory. When the information was in view and memory was not taxed, the older person performed well. When the information had to be remembered, the older person performed less well. The idea, then, is to keep as much information in front of the older person as possible when he or she carries out chores. Minimizing the burden on short-term memory can be helpful.

Abstract and Concrete Thought

There is another kind of help that can be provided to the elderly person in problem solving. If concepts and tasks are framed in practical, down to earth ways they will be better handled than when framed in less tangible, theoretical ways. If the task is concrete it will be more readily solved than when it is abstract.

Arenberg gave a problem to young and old adults with instructions to identify the important elements. The elements were in three categories: form, color, and number. The elements in the category form might have been a square, a circle, or a triangle; the color might have been red, blue, or yellow; number might have been one, two, or three. Arenberg presented one element from each category at one time. For example, he might present a circle, a red color, and the number three. This was called a trial. There were several trials and after each, Arenberg said yes or no. The yes and no information made it possible to identify the element Arenberg had targeted. For example, if a circle, red, and three was yes; and a circle, blue, and three was also yes, then either circle or three was yes. A trial of circle, red, and two was no, leaving three as the yes element, the element to be identified.

This is a very difficult task and the old people whom Arenberg tested did not do very well. But Arenberg himself was a problem solver and came up with an ingenious solution which made it possible for the older people to solve the problem.

Instead of abstract elements within the categories form, color, and number, he used concrete food items designated as beverage, meat, and vegetable. This constituted a meal instead of a trial. Arenberg told his problem solvers that one of the foods was poisoned, so instead of saying yes or no, he said died or lived. The task, instead of identification of the element, was now the identification of the poisoned food. For example, a meal of coffee (beverage), lamb (meat), and peas (vegetable) caused death because one of these three foods was poisoned. Another meal of coffee, veal and peas also caused death, thus coffee and peas remained as possibly poisoned foods. A meal of coffee, lamb, and corn, in not causing death, left peas as the poisoned food. Older people did relatively well with this problem, although they performed poorly in identifying the elements within abstract categories. In this way, Arenberg demonstrated that logic was only one dimension in the performances of older people. Age differences in problem-solving performance are more evident with abstract dimensions than with concrete ones.

One reason for this, perhaps, is that level of education is a factor in handling abstract ideas. Older people tend to have less schooling than the young, and artificial laboratory situations are often strange to them. An aid to the elderly, therefore, is to keep issues concrete. Older people not only handle such information more comfortably but one study also showed that, given a choice between solutions that were concrete but less good than abstract ones, and solutions which were abstract and good, many older people chose the concrete solutions.

Irrelevant Information

Another aid to the elderly in problem solving is to reduce irrelevant information as much as possible. Some information is not only irrelevant, it also actually gets in the way. Several studies, among them the poisoned food study, show this. In the example given before, knowing that either coffee or peas caused death, another meal of coffee, beef (not given before), and peas causing death conveys no further information and is irrelevant to solving the problem; it is redundant information. Arenberg found that such information gets in the way and hurts the old more than the young. Other studies working with very different types of tasks also found that redundant information is particularly bad for the older problem solver. Reducing the amount of redundant information helps the old very much.

Inquiry and Search

It is often necessary to ask for information in order to solve problems. A few studies show that older people made more inquiries in solving the problems than did younger people. The older people either needed more information to solve the problems or could not make sense of the information they got. Possibly, they forgot what they had learned in the inquiry.

Part of the reason, also, for making many inquiries is not knowing what the goal of the particular problem is. One study involved very difficult problems. Here, many of the older people did not seem to have explicit knowledge of the goal of the problem until very late. Their search for information was characterized by a lack of order and haphazard questioning rather than by concentration on a single path to the goal. This unordered search caused the information to be obtained only randomly, making it difficult to distinguish the relevant from the irrelevant. Before long, many participants were overwhelmed and confused by the many irrelevant facts and had to give up the task.

This confused behavior was noted only with very difficult tasks. Even so, it should not be taken as applying to all older people. It will be recalled that one study was longitudinal and age decline was not found until age 70, and then it was not large. This longitudinal study used the same type of difficult task used in the study where older people exhibited disorderly, haphazard search. If an aid to the elderly can be seen in these studies, it is to provide and keep the goal in the forefront of the problem solver's efforts. In this way, his inquiries and his searches for information could be orderly, systematically ignoring irrelevant information while moving toward the goal.

Teaching the Problem Solver

Recently, a new type of research has evolved. A new series of studies has focused not on comparing old and young but on teaching the old how to go about being successful in their efforts. The strategy in these teaching efforts has been to train people in the principles of the solution pattern, often starting with simple tasks and building up to more difficult ones. The general conclusion of these studies is optimistic. Not only are older people trainable but they also develop self-confidence in the process.

So many older people find the laboratory an alien, even frightening place that they seem to feel failure before they are far into the task. Training for solution success and the side effect of additional self-confidence is a hopeful new direction.

CREATIVITY AND CREATIVE PRODUCTIONS

Learning, memory, intelligence, problem solving—these abilities and mixtures of them may be expected to have a bearing on the creativity of people. In that extraordinarily creative people have been found to score high on intelligence tests, they do, but this has not accounted for their unusual abilities.

Outside the laboratory, in the world of work and career, creativity takes many forms. A recurring question is whether there is anything about creativity, whatever the form, that is different from extra good or high level skill. Is there anything really unique in the creative? The answer to this question bears on a controversy as to whether creativity falls with age.

Identifying Creativity

There has to be a public recognition of the creative person or the creative product or we would not know to label them as such. There are three major ways of identifying creative people or their products. One way is to get judgments by qualified experts; another is to develop tests of creativity and administer them, and the third is to refer to the frequency with which people or their work have been cited in the literature. An example of the first way is the ratings, by experts in various disciplines, of high school student projects submitted for national competition. The use of qualified experts rating professional people may be more difficult in that prominence can be confused with creativity. Prominence can result from frequent and popular solutions which are not necessarily creative.

An example of the use of test scores to identify the creative person can take the form of determining whose answers are most unique. Uniqueness and creativity, however, are not identical. Tests are also used to learn more about the creative person once he has been identified. Personality and other tests have shown that the creative person tends to be original, flexible, dedicated, and independent in thought and values. Intelligence is very often referred to, but more in the broad implications of problems rather than in small details. Creative people have been found to tolerate ambiguity and prefer complexity. They can live with conceptual disorder and need not impose organization immediately.

These descriptive statements come from the study of creative people after they have been identified in one way or another. The third way of identifying people, looking at cited references, has had the greatest bearing on the study of age and creativity. Some say that this method points to a lessening of creativity with age but others say it does not.

Age and Creativity

More than any other person, Lehman has studied the issue and found that creativity declines with age. Lehman provided information regarding the sciences, medicine, philosophy, arts, practical invention, and other areas. His method was to tabulate by age groups the frequency with which quality productions were listed in historical accounts. Often, he submitted the listings to university teachers for further evaluation.

One of his most important findings was that within most fields, the maximum rate of production for quality work was attained between the ages 30 to 39. This was earlier in life than the maximum for less distinguished work by the same people.

The rate of creative production did not decline rapidly after the peak years; instead, it declined gradually. It was more gradual for lesser quality products than for those of higher quality.

Lehman carefully showed that this 30 to 39 period was an overall average. The exact age varied from discipline to discipline and, more importantly, varied from person to person. A person can be great at any age.

Lehman's work was not without criticism. He was criticized by Dennis for combining the efforts of creative people who lived a long time with those who were short-lived. For example, if a man died at age 40, he could not produce after that period. If a man died at age 70, he could produce at any age up to 70. If the two are combined or averaged, it looks as though most of the work was done before age 40.

Dennis analyzed the productions only of people who lived long lives. His results showed that the peak years are to be found throughout most of the adult life span.

Dennis's and Lehman's results are hard to compare because Lehman emphasized superior quality and Dennis emphasized quantity. Dennis recognized this but insisted that it is difficult to arrive at an unbiased evaluation of quality.

This is the state of what we know. Does creativity decline with age? Maybe so, and if it does there are two reasons which can explain the decline. First, if we look back to the descriptions of the creative person, we can see that some of these seem to show a certain amount of change with age. Lehman suggested that a diminution of physical vigor and health may account for the decline, as may complacency, lowered motivation, and other factors. The second reason has nothing to do with ability or motivation.

As a creative, successful person ages, he is called upon to do a lot of important work that is not creative in the sense that it gets cited in the literature. He is given administrative and financial responsibilities; he becomes a teacher and counselor; he is sought after for advice. In other words, the percentage of creative working time that is available to him falls with age.

Thus, creativity may or may not fall with age. In either case, there are vast differences among people in creativity and at what age they express it. People can be great at any age.

GREAT AT ANY AGE

Possibly more than anyone else, Lehman was aware of the issues, pro and con, regarding age and creativity. He was aware of the argument that available creative research time diminishes when a person of note becomes older and more prominent. Lehman, however, brushed this argument aside, stating that it "would be well-nigh impossible" to measure accurately the amounts of time people of different ages devoted to research. Besides, he indicated, much creative thinking takes place when the person is not on the job and what is more, the thinker often is not aware of "thinking creatively."

Lehman was also aware of the argument of individual differences. In fact, in his book, *Age and Achievement*, he devotes a chapter to his subject entitled "Older Thinkers and Great Achievements." He listed, with very brief biographies, 94 persons who did notably creative work late in life, sometimes their most important work at that time. Twenty-nine of the 94 did work of note at 80 and over, the others at 70 and over. Some of this work could not have been created at an earlier age because it took nearly a lifetime to accumulate the necessary information.

Types of Accomplishments

Lehman concluded that, with exceptions, the work of old age differs from that done earlier in life. The creative work in old age is more likely to take the following forms:

1. preparation for publication of material used earlier in college lectures,

2. writing of personal memoirs,
3. recording and interpretation of what has been observed during most of a lifetime,
4. writing of important textbooks,
5. assembling of knowledge from a wide variety of fields,
6. completion or revision of work planned or begun earlier,
7. discussion of the problem of old age, and
8. writing of general and specialized histories.

In addition to creative accomplishments, older people have maintained roles of leadership with distinction. While Lehman believes that leadership positions are awarded on the basis of previous achievement, many people served late in life with much distinction. For example, several Supreme Court justices have served until past 80, with Holmes not retiring until 90. Gladstone was Prime Minister at 84. Churchill served as Prime Minister the second time from age 77 to 81. The peak age for leadership varies with the type of role, but often falls between the ages of 50 and 70.

Some Brilliant People
and Their Characteristics

Pressey and his wife reviewed Lehman's work and also an older listing by Hubbell, who provided an even broader list than Lehman's—a list of people who "performed distinctive service" after the age of 74. The Presseys then eliminated the ancients on the ground of insufficient evidence. Of the remaining persons, they selected those who had done important work at 80 or above, and who were important enough to be given three or more pages in the *Encyclopedia Britannica*. Nine names were selected in this way to which Churchill's was then added.

Michelangelo was the chief architect of St. Peter's from age 72 until his death at 89. Thomas Hobbes continued his brilliant writing career until his death at 91 and Voltaire still published at 83. Benjamin Franklin was influential until his death at 84 as was Thomas Jefferson at 83. Jefferson's last years were devoted to planning the University of Virginia. Goethe completed *Faust* at 82, and Victor Hugo was still writing after 80, as was Tennyson. And, as already noted, Gladstone and Churchill continued their brilliant political careers into their eighties.

The Presseys were convinced that these men, so varied in their careers, were not merely following through on achievements of earlier, prime years. Instead, they believed that some of these men did their greatest work beginning in their sixties. As varied as their work was, they had a lot in common. All, in their later years, had important perspectives on their work and their times; they had wide contacts and experience; they had tasted failure as well as success. They had loves and losses, hopes and disappointments—all had attained wisdom.

These great men had goals and purposes and they had the discipline needed to achieve them. Interestingly, the Presseys concluded that these goals and purposes in old age became increasingly benevolent. In their words, what characterized these ten men was their "wisdom and their persistent and powerful drive toward increasingly humanitarian achievements."

Not All Are Brilliant

Earlier, Pressey had wondered about the accomplishments of people aged 80 and older who were more ordinary in abilities and opportunities. "Do an appreciable number of them continue useful past 80?" he asked. He searched for material in case records, reports by university students, and clippings about older people. These three sources yielded a total of 290 persons aged 80 to 89 and 23 aged over 90.

These people, while more ordinary than the famous men written up in encyclopedias, are by no means ordinary. Their very long lives make them different, as does the fact that they were important enough to have been noted.

Most of these people aged 80 and above were working part time or occasionally, but a few were still working full time. Two men past 90 were active presidents of small town banks, another was a bank teller, a 90-year-old woman continued her insurance business. Pressey concluded that the accumulation of experience, knowledge, and wisdom which makes the greats especially valuable as leaders also makes the people of lesser ability extremely valuable. Opportunity is a keynote. Professional and self-employed people have had the greatest chance to continue their interests and this is why they are so strongly represented in Pressey's sample.

The point is that creativity or a lesser form of notable achievement is not necessarily limited to the young. If not greatness, or even recognized notable achievement, then at least continued usefulness and feelings of self-worth are possible at any age. Perhaps, creativity and achievement in old age should not be judged in terms of what has been done in the past but what is being done in the present. Given the opportunities for continued usefulness and self-respect, we are all capable of greatness in old age at our own levels.

REFERENCES

Arenberg, D. "Concept Problem Solving in Young and Old Adults." *Journal of Gerontology*, 1968, 23, 279-282.

Arenberg, D. "A Longitudinal Study of Problem Solving in Adults." *Journal of Gerontology*, 1974, 29, 650-658.

Botwinick, J. *Cognitive Processes in Maturity and Old Age.* Springer Publishing Co., New York, 1967. Chapter 7.

Botwinick, J. *Aging and Behavior.* Springer Publishing Co., New York, 1978. Chapter 14.

Brinley, J.F., Jovick, T.J., and McLaughlin, L.M. "Age, Reasoning, and Memory in Adults." *Journal of Gerontology*, 1974. 29, 182-189.

Dennis, W. "Age and Achievement: A Critique." *Journal of Gerontology*, 1956, 11, 331-333.

Dennis, W. "The Age Decrement in Outstanding Scientific Contributions: Fact or Artifact?" *American Psychologist*, 1958, 13, 457-460.

Hubbell, R.A. "Men and Women Who Have Performed Distinctive Service After the Age of 74." *Wilson Bulletin for Librarians*, 1935, 9, 297-304.

Jerome, E.A. "Decay of Heuristic Processes in the Aged." *Social and Psychological Aspects of Aging*, edited by C. Tibbitts and Wilma Donahue. Columbia University Press, New York, 1962.

Lehman, H.C. *Age and Achievement.* Princeton University Press, Princeton, N.J., 1953.

Lehman, H.C. "Reply to Dennis' Critique of Age and Achievement." *Journal of Gerontology*, 1956, 11, 333-337.

Pressey, S.L. "Jobs at 80." *Geriatrics*, 1958, 13, 678-681.

Pressey, S.L., and Pressey, A.D. "Genius at 80; and Other Oldsters." *Gerontologist*, 1967, 7, 183-187.

Rabbitt, P. "Changes in Problem Solving Ability in Old Age. *Handbook of the Psychology of Aging*, edited by J.E. Birren and K.W. Schaie. Van Nostrand Reinhold Co., New York, 1977.

Sanders, J.A.C., Sterns, H.L., Smith, M., and Sanders, R.E. "Modification of Concept Identification Performance in Older Adults." *Developmental Psychology*, 1975, 11, 824-829.

Chapter 14

When the End Comes

In the end, there is no choice; in the end, we die. We live, we age, and we know there is an end. The trick is to make living and aging as pleasant, as gratifying as possible, and to make death as acceptable as possible. In this book we have attempted to describe what happens in aging and the possibilities that are available to make aging pleasant and gratifying. Now, let us talk about death and see how we can make it as acceptable as the situation permits.

CLOSE IN MIND

Death is not far away in the minds of many older people. This is particularly true of people in the kind of nursing homes that provide around the clock custodial care. The residents are at least partially incapacitated because of mental or physical deterioration and they know that time is running out.

It is interesting—surprising, perhaps—that many such older people are not uncomfortable with the thought of death. They read obituaries and discuss death, much as younger people might discuss football games. Mealtime table talk might include "who went last night."

Much of what is known about attitudes toward death is based on terminally ill patients in hospitals. Little is known about attitudes of healthy old people residing in the community. There is reason to believe that many older adults also are ready to accept the end calmly. So frequently, it is the middle-aged son or daughter who cannot discuss death with their parents, while the parents can discuss it without emotion. They can talk about wills, burial plots, responsibilities, final wishes, and requests. They can accept the need for order in the arrangements regarding death.

Denial and Acceptance

The pioneering psychiatrist Kübler-Ross wrote that there is a general belief that death is a welcome friend to most of the aged. This is only partially true, she maintains, indicating that many old patients welcome death out of resignation rather than acceptance. Resignation sets in when life is no longer meaningful. There is no reason to believe that this is the case for non-institutionalized, healthy old people.

In Chapter 8, Erikson's stage theory was discussed. The last stage, ego-integrity, involves a final chance for self-acceptance. The old adult who successfully manages this stage must develop a sense of self-worth, a sense of order in life, and a sense of the inevitability of what happened before and what will happen in the future. What will happen, eventually, is death and it will be accepted without agony. Those among the elderly who do not successfully meet the crisis of ego-integrity find themselves in despair and in fear of dying. Most people do not end up in such despair; they accept the inevitability of death but want some control over the circumstances of the terminal phases.

How do the facts check out with Erikson's theory? In an extensive review of the literature Kastenbaum and Costa wrote: "Most studies of death attitudes in old age indicate the ability of well integrated people to accomodate themselves to finitude."

People distraught at the prospect of death experience stress. No two people react exactly alike to death and it is important to differentiate between the healthy, community-residing older person and the person who is very ill.

The Terminally Ill

Denial and Other Responses to Death. Four out of every five old people die in an institution such as a hospital, nursing home, or similar place, spending their last days there. Kübler-Ross interviewed many terminally ill patients and found a pattern common to all of them. First, she said, there is a denial of death. Her patients were of all ages, dying from a variety of causes. Perhaps it was for this reason that she saw so much denial when other investigators, working with older people not so close to death, did not report the same findings. Kastenbaum, for example, did not see denial as universal. Even in a "ward of chronically ill, life-threatened elderly," he pointed out, "people approach death in their own ways."

Denial of death is the first stage for Kübler-Ross. Then there are other stages. It is interesting to note that fear of death is not one of these. For many clinical investigators, fear of death is to be expected; it is natural. In fact, they maintain that if patients or other persons do not show fear, they are denying death. This may be true, but while many people may deny the reality of death, denial cannot be inferred from an absence of fear. Denial has to be inferred from a more direct basis. Actually, denial is not necessarily an either-or proposition. The psychologist Feifel wrote, "My own work with seriously ill patients . . . shows no necessary either-or-dichotomy . . . many hold simultaneous attitudes of both denial and acceptance of death."

Kübler-Ross continues from the first stage of denial to a second stage of *anger*. After the shock of learning that death is close subsides, anger and resentment take over. There is a feeling that the ordeal is unfair; people ask "Why me?" In their anger patients strike out at anyone at hand—doctors, nurses, or family. The next stage, according to Kubler-Ross, is *bargaining*. The dying person wants to strike a deal, perhaps with the physician, perhaps with God, with anyone. Soon, realizing the futility of this desire, *depression* sets in and may coincide with weakness and physical decline. Others think this state may have to do with the sedating drugs the patients are taking. Negative feelings, perhaps of guilt and worthlessness, set in. Finally the struggle is almost over. There is *acceptance* and less emotional pain. Fate has been accepted.

This stage patterning among the terminally ill—denial, anger, bargaining, depression, and acceptance—reflects an orderliness or regularity not seen by all investigators. There are other researchers who believe that individual adaptations to the process of dying are too varied to make them fit into a relatively simple stage sequencing.

The Doctor's Role. Kastenbaum points to an important fact: the doctor occupies a high status position and the old person a low status position. Once sick and dying, the elderly person is even more dependent and his status even lower. Further, the patient is in an institution without the usual supports of home and family. The whole experience is dehumanizing. Doctors need to be particularly sensitive about this, but the sad fact is that they are often just the opposite. Several investigators have noted that doctors avoid patients once they begin to die. One explanation for this conduct may be that a doctor's training has been focused on saving lives and not on caring for those who can no longer be saved. Also, doctors are people who, like so many of us, are not without anxiety and fear of death.

Kastenbaum points out that, ideally, the doctor not only pays close attention to the dying patient, providing what comfort and services he can, but also relates to the family of the patient. He should also relate to the nursing and other hospital staff who tender to the patient. The doctor should take the lead and set the pattern for acceptance of death and an ordering of the life that is coming to an end. Unfortunately, the busy doctor does not often see his role in this way. As a result of a busy schedule or financial considerations, he believes that other people should pick up the service role.

Should the Patient Be Told? The answer to this question is controversial. It is clear that most terminal patients want to be considered a whole person. Attempts by family members to lie about the state of the disease rarely succeed; they only confuse, anger, and depress the patient. Neither should the hospital staff pretend that everything is well. Let one inadvertent slip occur and the most careful plans are thrown into disorder.

Some investigators believe that the terminal patient somehow learns about his condition even if he is not directly told. Other investigators, however, maintain that many terminal patients remain unaware of their condition until death. It seems that most patients have some idea that they may not recover, but there is enough ambiguity to make for uncertainty. Schulz reviewed the literature on the question of whether the patient should be told unambiguously that there is no longer a way to sustain his life. One study made inquiries of patients and terminally ill patients, trying to ascertain whether they would want to know all the facts if terminally ill. The vast majority answered yes, but, interestingly, the dying patients had more no responses than the others. But even the terminally ill had a 67 percent yes response. Other studies with cancer patients revealed that the vast majority also wanted to know the facts. All these studies, of course, still do not tell us whether the patients should be told their prognoses; all we know is that the patients said they wanted to be told.

Another study compared dying patients with patients who were not dying. Among the dying, it was noted, those who showed awareness of their death were more depressed. Awareness may have caused the depression; on the other hand, the depression may have been caused by the physical distress of the more severe illness which results in death. Again, the answer to the question of telling the patient or not is unclear, even though the researcher concluded that it is better not to tell the patient, believing that knowing and depression go hand in hand. There is not enough data to answer the question with any authority. Still another study disclosed that while intense anxiety and depression resulted from learning the facts, these emotions dissipated in a short time with no apparent negative consequences.

Should the patient be told? It may come as a surprise to learn that physicians do not often inform patients of their condition.

Needs of the Patient. The patient, first of all, does not want to be abandoned. He does not want to lose contact with his loved ones and he does not want a different type of communication. He wants to retain his dignity and he wants the usual control of his world, as restrictive as it may have become. He can accept lessened independence but not the role of non-person.

If the patient is in pain, this has to be cared for. After this, his self-worth must be enhanced. He is a person with needs of love and attention. Many are afraid of being near a dying person, let alone having contact with him. Kübler-Ross, among others, has emphasized contact as very important to enhance a patient's feelings of self-worth and to indicate affection. Caress the dying loved one, hold him. The dying patient rarely has a catching disease and if he does, the doctors will quickly let you know. Listen to the patient, touch him, be with him. We should not be insensitive, however, to the fact that the patient also may show the need to be alone.

LOOKING TO THE END

Impending Death

Cognitive deterioration and personality change sometimes occur just before death comes and these can be seen as signs of warning. In Chapter 12 in connection with IQ test measurements, we discussed terminal drop, indicating that in the few years or months preceding death there seems to be an appreciable decline in test performance. It is not known whether this decline is due to sickness which precedes death or something else—a disorganizing, malfunctioning central nervous system, for example, or a disordered biochemistry which gave rise to the sickness. In any case, death often seems to be preceded by cognitive decline.

With such decline, often, there is confusion and agitation. Some older persons may draw away from others and spend much time seemingly preoccupied; others may continue much as usual. Those who withdraw seem to be the ones who find it hard to cope with people and events. Some seem to sense that death is close, others not.

Orderly Exit

There is now a vast literature on death and dying, much of it relating to the terminally ill patient, very little of it relating to the older person in relatively good health, residing in the community, and not thinking about death on a minute by minute basis. We do not know how frequent and pervasive the thoughts of death are among old people, nor how much planning is going on. We do not know what can or should be done to make the end or its prospect more acceptable. We are under the impression that older people are less afraid of death than younger people. In fact, Butler and Lewis report that older people are often more concerned about the death of loved ones than their own.

Sick, hospitalized patients and healthy, community residents alike want to plan and have control over leaving life in proper order. There are wills to make or to change, messages to leave and gifts to hand out personally. There are loved ones who need to be taken care of and children to be given a remembrance. There are funeral arrangements to be made.

All these arrangements take time to plan; they take thought.

Do people tend to do these things sufficiently far in advance? Can some of these functions be institutionalized to make the exit process more efficient and less painful? Should they be? Until the necessary research is undertaken, the answers to these and other important questions will have to be left unanswered.

REFERENCES

Butler, R.N. and Lewis, M.I. *Aging and Mental Health*. The C.V. Mosby Co., St. Louis, Mo., 1977. Chapter 3.

Feifel, H. Comments, part of a symposium entitled, "Attitude Toward Death in Older Persons: A Symposium." *Journal of Gerontology*, 1961, 16, 61-63. (Whole symposium pages 44-66.)

Kastenbaum, R. *Growing Old*. Harper and Row, New York, 1979. Chapter 10.

Kastenbaum, R. "The Physician and the Terminally Ill Patient." *Clinical Geriatrics*, 2nd Edition, edited by I. Rossman. J.B. Lippincott Co., Philadelphia, 1979.

Kastenbaum, R. and Aisenberg, R. *The Psychology of Death*. Springer Publishing Co., New York, 1976.

Kastenbaum, R. and Costa, P.T. "Psychological Perspectives on Death." *Annual Review of Psychology*, Vol. 27, edited by M.R. Rosenzweig and L.W. Porter. Stanford University Press, Palo Alto, Cal., 1977.

Kübler-Ross, E. *On Death and Dying*. Macmillan Publishing Co., New York, 1969.

Kübler-Ross, E. *Questions and Answers on Death and Dying*. Collier Books, New York, 1974. Chapter 11.

Chapter 15

Epilogue: Research Considerations[1]

What we know and understand from research is only as good as the methods and ideas we use. If our methods are no good, neither are our findings. If our ideas are barren or wrong, we will probably research the wrong propositions and arrive at the wrong conclusions. This chapter deals with methods and ideas about research on aging.

METHODS OF RESEARCH

Most of what we know about old age and aging is from observing older people and comparing them with younger ones. In other words, most of what we have learned from research is through the cross-sectional study. This method is flawed, but,

---

1. All the previous chapters were substantive, providing information about aging or the aged. This chapter deals with the ways data in research on the aging can be collected and what the data may mean.

    Many will find the chapter more difficult than the others. Moreover, not everyone is interested in research issues. For these reasons, the reader is advised to get what he or she can from this chapter but not get bogged down in such a way as to detract from having understood all that preceded.

unfortunately, other methods are also flawed. Since our methods are not perfect, neither are our conclusions. What we have learned from research, therefore, may need to be changed when new evidence becomes available.

Method in research has two meanings. One refers to the specific procedures used in measurement—the EEG apparatus used in measuring brain waves, for example. The other refers to the broader plan of the study, often described in terms of experimental design. It is the latter meaning which we will be discussing here.

There are three designs or types of study that are important for our present purposes: two involve age comparisons and one does not. The first two are the cross-sectional and the longitudinal method. The third employs what is called the time-lag.

Cross-Sectional Comparisons

Descriptive Versus Inferential Statements. The major fault with the cross-sectional method was pointed out in a talk by Robert Kastenbaum, now director of Cushing Hospital near Boston. He said,

> Occasionally I have the opportunity to chat with elderly people who live in the communities near by Cushing Hospital. I cannot help but observe that many of these people speak with an Italian accent. I also chat with young adults who live in these same communities. They do *not* speak with an Italian accent. As a student of human behavior and development I am interested in this discrepancy. I indulge in some deep thinking and come up with the following conclusion: as people grow older they develop Italian accents. This must surely be one of the prime manifestations of aging on the psychological level.

This tongue in cheek observation is humorous but it is also very serious about letting us know that many cross-sectional studies end up with conclusions of age change, when all that is really known is descriptive differences between old and young.

In fact, much of the material in this book which refers to decline, loss, and similar concepts of age change is really imprecisely, if not incorrectly, stated. The reason is that in this book, as in other books on aging, much of the content is based on observation of age difference and not on age loss or age decline.

The only incontrovertible statement that can be made on the basis of cross-sectional research is that of a difference between age groups born in different years. The inference of decline and loss may be wrong, just as was Kastenbaum's inference about the effect of aging on Italian accents. Nevertheless, we make inferences, realizing that we may be wrong because otherwise we would have no ideas about aging. We expect to make mistakes and we expect to correct them. Science proceeds from approximate truths to more accurate but still approximate truths.

Age and Cohort. It is easy, in the Kastenbaum observation, to infer that age does not bring on Italian accents. It is reasonable to infer that the elderly people grew up in a culture where English was not the primary or sole language spoken.

In most studies, it is not nearly as easy to separate generational or cultural-era effects from those of aging. Aging effects are thought to be biological in that they represent changes within the person, i.e., maturational changes. Cultural effects are called *cohort effects* by most investigators, with cohort being defined by the year of birth. It is thought that having been born in 1900, for example, makes for a very different cultural upbringing than having been born in 1960.

As indicated, these two effects, maturation and cohort, are so mixed together that they are hard to tell apart. For example, when intelligence test performances are lower in the elderly than the young, is this the result of maturational change or of cohort differences? Older cohorts have less schooling than younger cohorts and the educational level affects intelligence test performances.

The issue is even more complicated in that age or maturation really cannot be thought of in purely biological terms. We know that biological changes are dependent upon social conditions; aging, therefore, is not a totally biological function, it is also partly a social function. Aging cannot occur in the absence of a social context. For example, growth in children is biological, but without the proper social opportunity for nutrition and hygiene, growth is stunted, and disease ravages the body. Such biological and social aspects of aging define maturation. In any case, the cross-sectional method involves maturation and cohort and the mixing together of effects is called confounding. *Age and cohort effects are confounded in cross-sectional research.*

To repeat: Most of what we know about aging comes from cross-sectional studies and what we know, therefore, concerns group differences. We often make inferences of maturational change which might be wrong; the change may be in cohort, not in age.

Longitudinal Comparisons

The confounding of age and cohort has led some investigators to think that longitudinal research is the way around the problem. After all, they reason, if the same people are studied time and time again over the years, aging can be studied without the bothersome confounding of the cohort effect. This is true, but other problems arise, some of them looking very similar to the cohort effects in cross-sectional research.

Age and Time of Measurement. In 1954, Nelson carried out an interesting study. He tested college students with respect to the liberalism of their beliefs. He tested these same students again 14 years later and noted a marked trend to greater liberalism. Here is a longitudinal follow-up study, presumably designed to investigate age effects free from cultural or cohort effects. The conclusion to Nelson's study might have been that with aging, from college age to near middle age, liberalism increases.

Fortunately, Nelson did something unusual. At the time he gave his test the second time, he also gave it to a new group of college students. This new group made the same scores as did the older group when tested 14 years after the first test. The times had changed, making people more liberal. Aging did not do it, cultural changes did it. By convention, cultural changes that occur during the lifetime of the study are not called cohort effects but *time-of-measurement effects.*

Thus, cultural or environmental changes occur during the duration of a longitudinal study and these affect performance. These time-of-measurement effects are confounded with aging. *The problem with longitudinal research, therefore, is the confound between the effects of age and those of time-of-measurement.* (As mentioned in Chapter 12, psychologists speak of time-of-measurement effects, while sociologists call them period effects.)

Time-of-measurement effects are not limited to changes in the social environment alone. They may include personal and physical changes as well. For example, personal changes may include motivation. If a person taking the test is highly motivated the first time but not the second time, the change in test performance may be due more to this fact than to aging. Similarly, if the person is sick at the second testing, the change in health rather than age may be the factor. An example of another type of change is seen in the physical environment. There may be a change in the equipment that was used in testing. If, at the time of the second testing, the equipment is calibrated or adjusted differently from the first testing, the performances will be seen as different and will mistakenly be attributed to age changes.

Advantages and Disadvantages. Longitudinal research has many virtues despite the time-of-measurement effects. First, these effects are not likely to be as important or as large as the cohort effects in cross-sectional research. Second, the longitudinal method is the only method that enables us to go back to the data of the first testing to see what might be related to the later performances and happenings. For example, it was mentioned in Chapter 12 that after several different longitudinal intelligence studies had been completed, the early test performances were examined to see if they could have been used as predictors of deaths which occurred later.

A third advantage to a longitudinal study is that it is the only method that allows us to chart changes over time for the individual person. It not only permits charting of average changes, but it also permits analysis of the amount of variation a person shows within a single test session. For example, if a person is very variable at a present test session but was hardly variable during earlier sessions, the investigator might start looking for something wrong. It may be something as transient as a change in motivation or something more enduring, such as cardiovascular problems. With hardening or narrowing of the arteries there are blood pressure changes which cause variations in the blood supply to the brain, resulting in possible variations in performance.

These are the important advantages derived from longitudinal research but there are some important disadvantages also. First, there is the sampling problem of selective subject dropout: the less able drop out as the research continues over the years. Thus, the longitudinal investigation, after a while, no longer is a representative or random sampling of people who are being studied, but a biased sample of mainly those who scored well initially. This can make for faulty conclusions with regard to the broader, general population.

Other disadvantages of longitudinal studies are that they are costly and require much patience and time. The investigator has to commit years to the study and has to stay with examination procedures which may have gone out of general use. In order to carry out a longitudinal investigation properly, mistakes and poor decisions made years ago have to be continued.

It is unlikely, therefore, that we will see a larger percentage of longitudinal studies in the future than we did in the past. Most of what we know now comes from cross-sectional studies, and we may expect it to remain so in the future.

Time-Lag Comparisons

Time-lag studies bear on aging but only indirectly. Time-lag comparisons involve two or more groups of the same age. In Nelson's study, it will be recalled, there were three testings: (1) a first college group test, (2) the same group tested 14 years later, and (3) a new college group tested for the first time, 14 years after the initial college group had been tested. The time-lag comparison concerns the two college groups of the same age, tested 14 years apart.

Cohort and Time-of-Measurement. Time-lag comparisons are important to age comparisons because they help us understand test results. It will be recalled that the 14-year longitudinal comparison taken alone suggested an age effect, i.e., from college age to middle age people became more liberal. However, this was seen as wrong once the time-lag comparison was made. The time-lag comparison shows that there was a time-of-measurement effect during the 14-year course of the study. The social environment had changed and had affected people's beliefs.

Time-lag comparisons involve time-of-measurement (or period) effects. They also involve another effect—that of cohort. The second college group was born 14 years later than the first group. The two groups were of the same college age but of a different cohort (born at different times). If all we knew was that the two college age groups were different, we would not know whether to attribute this to their different early-life (cohort) upbringing or to the time-of-measurement effect. However, knowing that the longitudinal result (which does not involve cohort but does involve time-of-measurement) made for the same result as the time-lag (which involves both cohort and time-of-measurement), the logical interpretation is one of time-of-measurement effect because it is common to both types of analyses. In summary, then, *the confound in time-lag studies is between cohort and time-of-measurement effects.*

Interpretations. There are two relatively recent studies in which time-lag comparisons were made in conjunction with longitudinal comparisons with interesting interpretations. These two studies demonstrate how more knowledge of the three confounded variables (age, cohort, and time-of-measurement) can lead to better understanding of what seems to be happening.

The first study is by Woodruff and Birren, who had acquired the results of an investigation of college students taking a test in 1944. The students were then between 19 and 20 years old and took a test called the California Test of Personality. Twenty-five years later, in 1969, many of these now ex-college students were given the test again. They were between 44 and 45 years old at the time of the second testing. Woodruff and Birren found the personality scores were just about the same in 1969 as they were in 1944. Since such longitudinal comparisons confound age and time-of-measurement, and since the longitudinal comparison disclosed no change in personality, it may be concluded that personality was not related to either age or time-of-measurement.[2]

In 1969, at the time Woodruff and Birren tested the alumni the second time, they also tested new college students for the first time. They now had a time-lag study comparing 19 to 20-year-olds of 1944 with 19- to 20-year-olds in 1969. Here they found a difference: The 1944 college students scored more highly than the 1969 college students in self- and social adjustment. Time-lag comparisons confound cohort and time-of-testing. If we concluded from the longitudinal part of the study that time-of-testing is not a factor in personality change, we would conclude that the difference between the 1944 and 1969 students was due to cohort effects. The differences in the students' personalities may be attributed to the differences in their respective upbringings. There was a generational difference. Their cultural milieus were different and the shorthand way for accounting for it is the cohort effect. In other words, age and time-of-measurement were ruled out, leaving cohort.

The second study is similar in some ways but with an extra result which made for a unique interpretation. Whitbourne and Waterman also tested college students, the first time in 1966

---

2. This conclusion may be wrong because, conceivably, the effects of age and time-of-measurement could be opposite. For example, age could improve personality over the 25 years and time-of-measurement could make it worse. These two effects combine or average out to show no change over the 25 years. The conclusion of no effect of either age or time-of-measurement, however, is parsimonious.

and the second time 10 years later, in 1976. They gave a test called the Inventory of Psychosocial Development and found that there had been a significant development over these 10 years. This is a longitudinal study. Was the change due to age? To time-of-measurement? Or to both?

Then, Whitbourne and Waterman tested a group of college students for the first time in 1976 and compared them to the 1976 alumni. The alumni, the older people, were found to be more psychosocially developed. This was a cross-sectional comparison. Was the development due to maturation? To cohort? Or both?

Next, the 1976 college students were compared to the 1966 college students—a time-lag comparison. There was no difference. Since cohort and time-of-measurement are the confounds in time-lag comparisons, it might have been concluded that neither of them were important in development, leaving age as the only factor.

Whitbourne and Waterman, however, also found that the time-lag comparison was different for men and women. The 1976 women were more psychosocially developed than the 1966 women; on the other hand, the 1976 men were less developed than the 1966 men. The interpretation was that since the time-lag effect for men was to make for poorer development (1976 college men less developed than 1966 college men) while both the cross-sectional and longitudinal comparisons (1976 versus 1966) showed greater development with time, age must be the basis for the change (since cohort and time-of-measurement worked to retard development). With women, however, since time-of-measurement improved development, the improvement —seen cross-sectionally and longitudinally—may have been only partially due to age, if it was due to age at all.

This is a complicated interpretation and it shows that simple age comparisons may not disclose what is actually going on, which brings us to a point made at the beginning of the chapter: in research on aging we are often left uncertain about what age comparisons mean. Even the complicated studies described above leave us with some uncertainty. Differences can be due to cohort, time-of-measurement, age, or combinations of all three. We often infer that one of these is important, knowing that we may be wrong but hoping that if we are, future research will show us the way to obtain more correct inferences.

TESTS AND INDIVIDUAL DIFFERENCES

Tests of all kinds are given to people of different ages and inferences are made regarding age differences and age changes. Even if our inferences are correct about the effects of age, it is always in order to ask "so what?"

In Chapter 12, we discussed intellectual ability in relation to age, with an emphasis on what tests of intelligence mean. We pointed out that it is absolutely crucial to pay attention to the purpose of the test and to decide whether the test fulfills the purpose. The example given was that if a test of intelligence is a good predictor of school performance, and a 70-year-old gets a low score on the test, what does it matter?

Functional assessment, be it behavioral or physiological, needs to be considered in relation to the needs and life habits of a person. Even something as basic as eye cataracts, for example, can be evaluated in relation to need. The prescription of a surgical operation may be different for a person who reads a lot or is involved in close work, needlepoint, for example, than for a person who spends much of his time sitting in small groups conversing. Functional loss is meaningful to a person largely in terms of need and lifestyle.

There is one more point we have made many times in this book, and one that can hardly be overemphasized: people are different from one another, and this is even more true of the elderly than the young. Some old people perform better than some young people on almost any given task. In addition, there is overlap between the young and the old.

When old and young are compared, it is almost always the

average score of the elderly that is compared with the average score of the young. The averages combine all the individual differences and fail to show us the overlap. One study attempted to focus on the overlap and concluded: "We wage that, if all age comparisons were made on the basis...[of the overlap] not the average scores, much of the age difference which may seem impressive at first would lose its interest."

There are deficits with age but let us never forget the great abilities that remain. Let us not forget the benefits of long years of experience. There are many contributions and services to be expected from the aging and the aged until very late in life.

REFERENCES

Botwinick, J. *Aging and Behavior.* Springer Publishing Co., New York, 1978. Chapters 19 and 20.

Botwinick, J. and Thompson, L.W. "Age Difference in Reaction Time: An Artifact?" *Gerontologist,* 1968, 8, 25-28.

Nelson, E.N.P. "Persistence of Attitudes of College Students Fourteen Years Later." *Psychological Monographs,* 1954, 68, 1-13.

Whitbourne, S.K. and Waterman, A.S. "Psychosocial Development During the Adult Years: Age and Cohort Comparisons." *Developmental Psychology,* 1979, 15, 373-378.

Woodruff, D.S. and Birren, J.E. "Age Changes and Cohort Differences in Personality." *Developmental Psychology,* 1972, 6, 252-259.

Index